Chess Traveller's Quiz Book

By

Julian Hodgson
International Grandmaster

CADOGAN CHESS
LONDON, NEW YORK

CADOGAN BOOKS DISTRIBUTION

UK/EUROPE/AUSTRALASIA/ASIA/AFRICA
Distribution: Grantham Book Services Ltd, Isaac Newton Way, Alma
park Industrial Estate, Grantham, Lincs NG31 9SD
Tel: (0476) 67421 Fax: (0476) 590223

USA/CANADA/LATIN AMERICA/JAPAN
Distribution: Macmillan Distribution Center, Front and Brown Streets,
Riverside, New Jersey 08075, U.S.A.
Tel: (609) 461 6500 Fax: (609) 764 9122

Library of Congress Cataloguing-in-Publication Data
(applied for)

British Library Cataloguing-in-Publication Data
A CIP catalogue record for this book is available from the British
Library

Hodgson, Julian
    Chess Traveller's Quiz Book
    I. Title
    794.1
    ISBN 1-85744-030-7

Typeset in Great Britain by Philmar DTP Services, Oxfordshire
Printed in Great Britain by BPCC Wheatons Ltd, Exeter

Introduction

The aim of this book is twofold: firstly to be instructive and secondly — and more importantly — to be enjoyable.

All the puzzles have been taken from positions that have actually arisen in tournament games. They have been placed roughly in order of difficulty (although, of course, this is purely a subjective opinion — i.e. mine!) beginning with the easiest and then becoming progressively harder and harder. Occasionally I have thrown in a slightly easier set to stop you, the reader, from becoming too bogged down in analysing long, complicated variations.

As the book is aimed at a wide range of players, from beginner right through to grandmaster, do not be too disheartened if you struggle with the first few — you will improve as you progress through the book (honest!).

Why has it been called a traveller's quiz book you might ask? Well, from my own personal experience, there is nothing quite as frustrating as having a train or plane (or any other form of transport for that matter!) delayed and then having absolutely nothing to do to occupy one's mind — this book should put an end to that potential problem!

Advice on Exercises

Enjoy them! But, seriously, they are arranged in groups of four with the solutions overleaf. Try to work out as much as you can before looking at the solutions.

For most positions you can score a maximum 5 points with an occasional ten-pointer thrown in. Thus for the first set of four positions you can score a maximum 20 points; but to score full marks you must have seen all the relevant variations and also have worked them out in the allotted time (in the first set it would be six minutes or less). I leave it to your discretion as to how many points you think you deserve.

If this all sounds too complicated or like too much hassle, then I suggest you just enjoy looking at the positions and some of the beautiful moves that are needed to solve them.

Good Luck! (And don't forget to catch the train!).

Chapter One

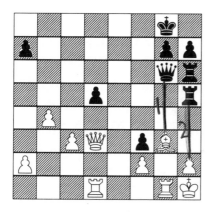

1 Isahor–Pichelaury
USSR 1978
Black to play and win

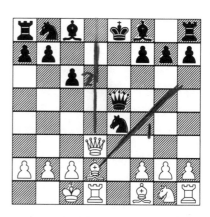

2 Reti–Tartakower
Vienna 1923
White to play and win

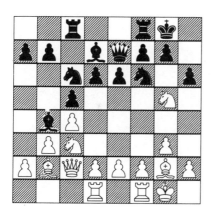

3 Uhlmann–Schwarz
East Germany 1975
White to play and win

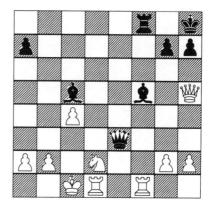

4 Jacobs–Gallagher
London 1987
Black to play and win

Solutions

1 1 ... ♕xg3! 2 ♖xg3 (or 2 ♕xd5+ ♖xd5 3 fxg3 ♖xh2+! 4 ♔xh2 ♖h5 mate) 2 ... ♖xh2+ 3 ♔g1 ♖h1 mate. **5 points** — only **3 points** if you missed the win against 2 ♕xd5+.

2 1 ♕d8+ ♔xd8 2 ♗g5+! ♔c7 3 ♗d8 checkmate, (or 2 ... ♔e8 3 ♖d8 checkmate) **5 points.** Watch out for this idea — it will crop up again!

3 1 ♘d5! exd5 2 ♗xf6 wins the queen or forces mate on h7. **5 points.**

4 1 ... ♕c3+! 2 bxc3 ♗a3 mate. **5 points.** No credit for 1 ... ♗a3 as 2 ♕f3 defends.

Short and sharp — although the killer blow usually is in chess! Well done if you passed this initiation unscathed, but do not be too downhearted if you didn't — you will improve. *Deduct* 1 point for every minute spent over six minutes. 20 points maximum. (Thus ten minutes for a correct solution earns 20-4=16 points).

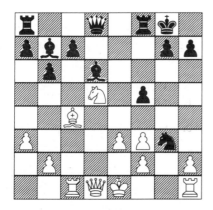

5 Johnson–Marshall
Chicago 1899
White to play and win

6 Schulten–Horwitz
London 1846
Black to play and win

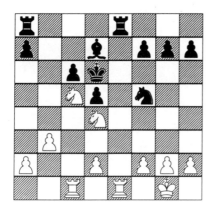

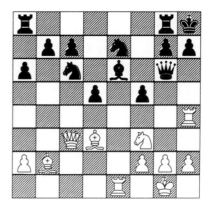

7 Locasto–Zacrzewski
Poland 1974
White to play and win

8 Shishkov–Saltayev
USSR 1986
White to play and win

Solutions

5 1 ♘e7+ ♔h8 2 ♘g6+! hxg6 3 hxg3+ ♕h4 4 ♖xh4 mate. **5 points**. Only 3 points for 1 ♘f4+ as Black can struggle on with 1 … ♖f7 — try to be clinical in your finishing.

6 1 … ♕f1+! 2 ♔xf1 ♗d3+ (Double discovered check is an incredibly powerful weapon). 3 ♔e1 ♖f1 checkmate. **5 points**.

7 1 ♘b5+! cxb5 2 ♘b7 mate. Short and sweet — although possible to miss in a game. **5 points**.

8 1 ♖xe6 ♕xe6 2 ♘g5 ♕g6 3 ♖xh7+! ♕xh7 4 ♘f7 checkmate. This mate is called a smothered mate and occurs more often in chess than you might think — well done if you spotted it. **5 points**. Only **2 points** if you missed the mate and played 2 ♖xh7+ ♔xh7 3 ♘g5+.

Another set of snap finishes. 20 points maximum. *Deduct* 1 point for every minute over five minutes.

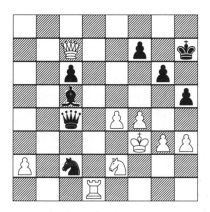

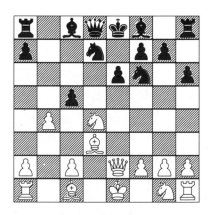

9 Ivanovsky–Lyustrov
Moscow 1972
Black to play and win

10 Perenyi–Eperjesi
Hungary 1974
White to play and win

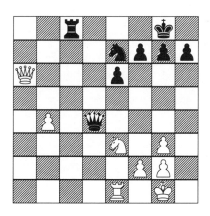

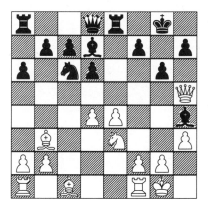

11 Hmelnitsky–Kabiatansky
USSR 1989
White to play and win

12 Lind–Olsson
Malmo Open 1976
White to play and win

Solutions

9 1 ... ♛d3+! 2 ♖xd3 (If 2 ♔g2 ♛xe2+ and wins) 2 ... ♞e1 mate. **5 points.** A pretty finish.

10 1 ♞c6 ♛c7 (or ♛b6) 2 ♛xe6+! fxe6 3 ♗g6 mate. **5 points**.

11 1 ♞f5! exf5 (1 ... ♛f6 2 ♞xe7+; 1 ... ♞xf5 2 ♛xc8+) 2 ♛xc8+ ♞xc8 3 ♖e8 mate. **5 points** — this is quite a hard one as it is not immediately apparent from the initial position that White's rook will deliver mate within a couple of moves. Well done, if you saw it.

12 1 ♗xf7+! ♔xf7 2 ♛xh7+ ♔f8 (2 ... ♔e6 3 d5+ wins) 3 ♞f5 followed by 4 ♗h6+ or 1 ♗xf7+ ♔g7 2 ♛h6+ ♔xh6 3 ♞f5+ ♔h5 4 g4 mate (or 4 ♞g7 mate). 1 ♗xf7+ ♔h8 2 ♗xg6 also leaves White with a winning position. **1 point** for 1 ♗xf7+, plus **1 point** for seeing 1 ... ♔xf7 2 ♛xh7+, plus **3 points** for 1 ... ♔g7 2 ♛h6+. Total, **5 points.** If you worked out all of the above you are a better calculator than me. (Or you have been cheating!)

This is a harder set — the pace is hotting up even if the tube isn't. 20 points maximum. *Deduct* 1 point for each minute over ten minutes.

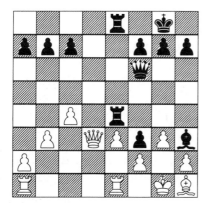

13 Carls–Acers
USA 1981
Black to play and win

14 Oliveira–Pereira
Portugal 1974
Black to play and win

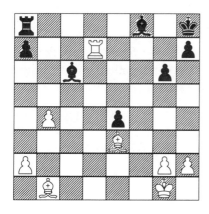

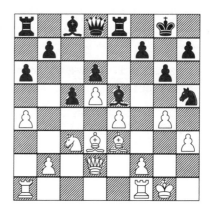

15 Ivanka–Polihroniade
Budapest 1977
White to play and win

16 Calderin–Sariego
Manzanillo 1991
Black to play and win

Solutions

13　1 ... ♖xe3! 2 ♕xe3 ♖xe3 3 ♖xe3 ♕xa1+ or 1 ... ♖xe3 2 ♕xe3 ♖xe3 3 fxe3 f2 mate. **4 points**, plus **1 point** if you planned to meet 2 ♕d2 with either 2 ... ♕b2 or 2 ... ♖e2.

14　1 ... ♘e4+! 2 ♔xe3 ♕g5+ 3 ♔xe4 ♖e8+ 4 ♔d4 ♕e5+ 5 ♔c4 ♗e6+ 6 ♔b4 ♖b8+ 7 ♔a3 ♕d6+ 8 b4 ♕xb4 mate, or 7 ♔a4 ♕b5+ 8 ♔a3 ♕b4 mate or, 3 ♔d4 ♖d8+ 4 ♔c4 ♕d5+ 5 ♔b4 ♖b8+. **3 points** for seeing as far as 3 ... ♖e8+, plus **2 points** for seeing 4 ... ♕e5+ 5 ♔c4 ♗e6+, Black must be careful not to allow the king to escape via e3 or c3. If you saw right to the end after 1 ... ♘e4+ you have done exceedingly well as it is so easy for the opponent's king to wriggle out — one wrong check and suddenly you are several pieces down for nothing.

15　1 ♗d4+ ♔g8 2 a3!! (threatening 3 ♗a2+) 2 ... ♔h6 3 ♗a2+ ♔f8 4 ♖c7 ♗b5 5 ♖xh7 followed by 6 ♖h8+. **5 points** for seeing as far as 3 ♗a2+. Only **4 points** if you chose the less accurate 2 a4 or 2 ♗c2, allowing 2 ... ♗xb4. 2 a3!! is a so-called 'quiet move' and as a result very hard to see — don't be too discouraged if you missed it — so did I!

16　1 ... ♕h4 2 gxh5 (2 ♔g2 ♗xg4 3 hxg4 ♕xg4+ 4 ♔h1 ♕h3+ 5 ♔g1 ♕h2 mate) 2 ... ♗h2+ 3 ♔xh2 ♕xh3+ 4 ♔g1 ♕g4+ 5 ♔h1 (5 ♔h2 ♖e5 threatening ... ♖h5+) 5 ... ♕f3+ 6 ♔h2 ♖e5 — Swinging a rook into the attack is a common theme in many chess combinations. White resigned. **5 points**.

Getting more difficult. 20 points maximum. *Deduct* 1 point for each minute over twelve minutes.

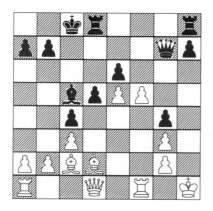

17 Becher–Bruckner
West Germany 1985
Black to play and win

18 Schiffers–Tchigorin
Berlin 1897
Black to play and win

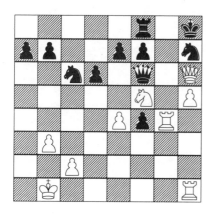

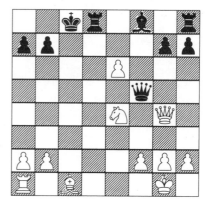

19 Bach–Botto
Tjentiste 1975
White to play and win

20 Shashin–Kolevit
USSR 1974
White to play and win

Solutions

17   1 ... ♕g6! (threatening 2 ... ♕h5 mate) 2 fxg6 hxg6+ mating. **5 points**. No credit for 1 ... ♕f7?? 2 ♕xg4.

18   1 ... ♖h1+! 2 ♘xh1 ♗h2+ 3 ♔xh2 ♖h8+ 4 ♔g3 ♘f5+ 5 ♔f4 or g4 ♖h4 mate. **5 points**. Either you see it or you don't! Tchigorin missed it, but of course you have the advantage of knowing the win is there.

19   1 ♖g6! fxg6 (1 ... ♕e5 2 ♖g7 or, more spectacularly, 2 ♕xh7+ wins). 2 hxg6 ♖f7 3 ♕f8+! (3 gxf7 ♕xf7 is much slower) 3 ... ♖xf8 4 ♖xh7+ ♔g8 5 ♘h6 mate. **4 points** for seeing 1 ♖g6 and an additional point for 3 ♕f8+.

20   1 ♗f4! ♕xg4 2 ♖c1+ ♗c5 3 ♖xc5 mate. **5 points**. *Deduct* 3 points for 1 ♕xf5?? ♖xd1 mate.

Did you catch number 18? The position, not the bus! A maximum of 20 points. *Deduct* 1 point for each minute over ten minutes.

Chapter Two

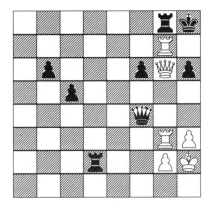

21 Moonen–Euwe
Holland 1981
Black to play and win

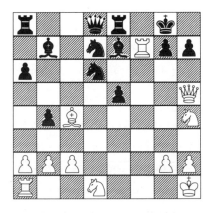

22 Kaplan–Heinrich
USA 1974
White to play and win

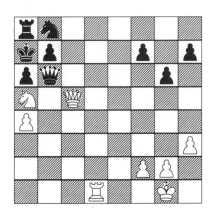

23 Farago–Bjerring
West Germany 1989
White to play and win

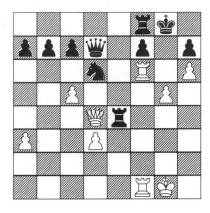

24 Basman–Balshan
Israel 1981
White to play and win

Solutions

21 1 ... ♖xg2+! 2 ♔xg2 ♕xg3+ 3 ♕xg3 (or 3 ♔xg3) 3 ... ♖xg7 wins back the queen and reaches a winning pawn endgame. **5 points**.

22 1 ♖f8+ By now you should be spotting the deadly double-discovered check! 1 ... ♔xf8 2 ♘g6+! hxg6 3 ♕h8 mate. **5 points**. 1 ♘f5, **3 points**, also wins, for example 1 ... ♘xf5 2 ♖f8+ ♔xf8 3 ♕f7 mate, but it is always good technique to find the most forcing, most clearcut line.

23 1 ♖b1! ♘d7 (If 1 ... ♕xc5 2 ♖xb7 mate) 2 ♕d4 (or 2 ♕e3) wins the queen. **3 points** for 1 ♖b1, **2 points** for seeing 1 ... ♘d7 and its refutation.

24 1 ♖g6+! fxg6 (1 ... hxg6 2 ♕g7 mate) 2 ♕h8+! ♔xh8 3 ♖xf8 mate. **5 points**. No credit for 1 dxe4? ♕g4+.

Elegant, but reasonably straightforward. 20 points maximum. *Deduct* 1 point for each minute over eight minutes.

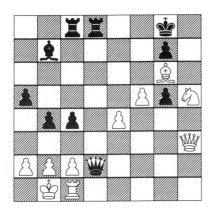

25 Westyn–Fridriksson
Sweden 1973
Black to play and win

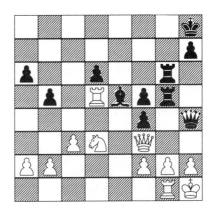

26 S. Pereira–R. Pereira
Portugal 1978
Black to play and win

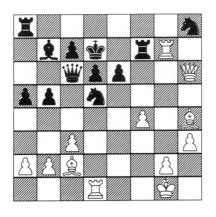

27 Musolino–Siveri
Catandggiaro 1970
White to play and win

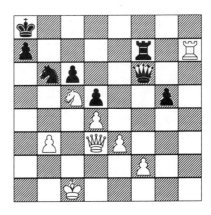

28 Katalimov–Kolpakov
Riga 1975
White to play and win

Solutions

25 1 ... ♕xc2+! 2 ♖xc2 ♖d1+ 3 ♖c1 ♗xe4+ 4 ♔a1 ♖xc1 mate or 2 ♔xc2 ♗xe4+ 3 ♕d3 ♗xd3+ 4 ♔d2 ♗xf5+ 5 ♔ moves ♗xg6. **5 points**. In the second line, you need only have seen as far as 2 ... ♗xe4+ for full credit.

26 1 ... ♖g3! 2 fxg3 ♕xh2+ 3 ♔xh2 ♖h6+ and mates. **5 points**. But absolutely no credit for the hasty 1 ... ♕xh2+?? 2 ♔xh2 ♖h6+ 3 ♕h3 and White wins!

27 1 ♕xe6+! ♔xe6 2 ♖e1+ ♘e3 (2 ... ♔d7 3 ♗f5 mate) 3 ♖xe3+ ♔d5 4 ♖g5+ ♔c4 5 ♗b3 mate (or 5 b3 mate, or 5 ♗d3 mate). There is nothing quite like a good king hunt! **5 points**. Nothing if you inserted 1 ♖xf7+ ♘xf7 before playing 2 ♕xe6+ ♔xe6 3 ♖e1+; if nothing else, 3 ... ♘e5 wins for Black.

28 1 ♕g6! ♕xg6 (or 1 ... ♖f8 2 ♕xf6 ♖xf6 3 ♖h8+ and mates or 1 ... ♕xf2 2 ♖h8+ (the most accurate) 2 ... ♖f8 3 ♕e8+! and mates. **5 points.**

A bit of care needed to avoid false trails. 20 points maximum. *Deduct* 1 point for each minute over 5 minutes.

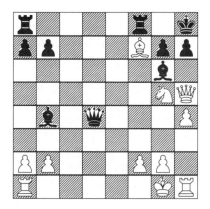

29 Sibarevic–Pavlov
Pernik 1988
White to play and win

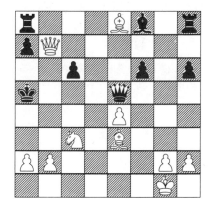

30 Toth–Nemet
Switzerland 1984
Black to play and win

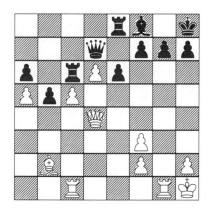

31 Plachetka–Tibensky
Trnava 1988
White to play and win

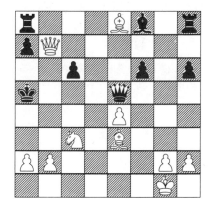

32 Plaskett–Tarsh
Bath 1984
White to play and win

Solutions

29 1 ♕xg6 hxg6 2 h5! ♖xf7 3 hxg6+ ♔g8 4 gxf7+ ♔f8 5 ♘e6+ ♔xf7 6 ♘xd4 wins material. **5 points**, but only **3 points** if you had not considered 2 ... ♖xf7.

30 1 ... ♖xf1+ 2 ♔xf1 (2 ♖xf1 ♘h3+ followed by ... ♕xe4) 2 ... ♘h3+ 3 ♕f3 or ♖f3 ♕f2+! 4 ♕ or ♖xf2 ♖xf2 mate. **5 points**. The final sacrifice is attractive, and only **3 points** if you had missed it. The real problem though is rejecting the alternatives. No credit for 1 ... ♘e2+ as White is ahead in material after 2 ♕xe2 ♖xe2 3 ♖xe2. **2 points** for 1 ... ♘h3+, but White has 2 ♔h2!, forcing Black to find 2 ... ♘f4+ 3 ♔g1 ♖xf1+) — All in all quite a confusing position.

31 1 ♕xg7+! ♗xg7 2 ♗xg7+ ♔g8 3 ♗f6+ ♔f8 4 ♖g7 intending 5 ♖cg1 or 5 ♖xh7 followed by mate. White even meets 4 ... ♕d8 with 5 ♖cg1. **2 points** for finding the sacrifice; **2 points** more for following the combination through and a **bonus point** if you saw that 1 ♖xg7 fails to 1 ... e5! 2 ♖xh7+ ♔xh7 3 ♕h4+ ♗h6 (not 3 ... ♔g8? 4 ♖g1+ ♗g7 5 ♕f6! when it is White who is winning) and Black wins.

32 1 b4+ ♗xb4 2 ♗b6+! axb6 3 ♕xa8 mate. **5 points**. 1 ♗b6+ wins also after 1 ... axb6 2 ♕xa8+ ♔b4 3 ♕a4+, etc; but it's messy and long-winded, so only **2 points**.

Getting more difficult now. Even a master would start to struggle. 20 points maximum. *Deduct* 1 point for each minute over fifteen minutes.

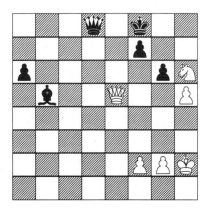

33 From–Hoi
Veilby 1976
White to move and win

34 Steinikov–Jaskoy
USSR 1988
White to play and win

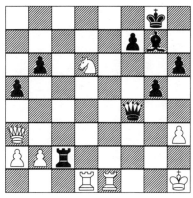

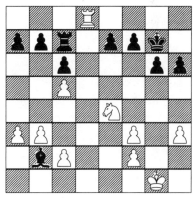

35 Vidmar–Euwe
Carlsbad 1929
White to play and win

36 Peresipkin–Chekhov
USSR 1976
White to play and win

Solutions

33 1 ♕h8+ ♚e7 2 ♘f5+! gxf5 3 ♕xd8+ ♚xd8 4 h6 and the pawn touches down. **5 points**. This position is actually quite a difficult one as it is not so easy to visualise from the initial position that the h5 pawn will queen.

34 1 ♕xg7+! ♚xg7 2 ♖g4+ ♚h6 (2 ... ♚h8 3 ♗f6 mate) 3 ♖d6+ f6 (3 ... ♚h5 4 ♖h4 mate) 4 ♖xf6+ ♚h5 5 ♖h4+ ♚xh4 6 ♖h6 mate or 5 ... ♚g5 6 f4+ ♚xh4 7 ♖h6 mate. **3 points** for the queen sacrifice; **2 points** extra if you saw the rook sacrifice as well.

35 1 ♖e8+ ♗f8 (1 ... ♚h7 2 ♕d3+ and 3 ♕xc2) 2 ♖xf8+! ♚xf8 3 ♘f5+ ♚g8 4 ♕f8+! ♚xf8 5 ♖d8 mate. **5 points**. You had to see the queen sacrifice. If you chose 4 ♖d8+ instead, only **2 points**; Black has 4 ... ♚h7 5 ♖h8+ ♚g6.

36 1 ♘d6 (threatening the fork 2 ♘e8+) 1 ... exd6 2 cxd6 and Black's rook is trapped. **5 points**. A nice little one-mover for the journey home.

20 points maximum. *Deduct* 1 point for each minute over ten minutes.

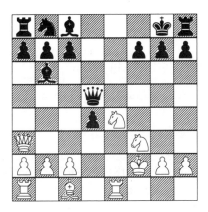

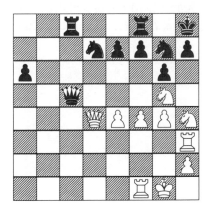

37 Richardson–Delmar
USA 1850
White to play and win

38 Perez Garcia–Zecevic
Pula 1986
White to play and draw

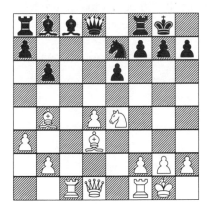

39 Wibe–Schneider
Norway v. Sweden 1975
White to play and win

40 Bjornland–Valtysson
Norway 1978
White to play and win

Solutions

37 1 ♘f6+! gxf6 2 ♕f8+! ♔xf8 3 ♗h6+ ♔g8 4 ♖e8 mate. **5 points**.

38 1 ♕xh6 ♕xe1+ 2 ♗f1 ♕c3 (2 ... ♖g8 loses to 3 ♕xh7+) 3 ♕xh7+! ♔xh7 4 ♖h6+ ♔g8 5 ♘e7+ ♔g7 6 ♘f5+ etc. **5 points**. Not 1 ♖xh6 since 1 ... ♕xe1+ 2 ♗f1 ♘f6 gives Black a breathing space to win with his extra material. Only **1 point** for 1 ♖xh6.

39 1 ♘f6+! gxf6 (1 ... ♔h8 2 ♘xh7 and 3 ♕h5 wins) 2 ♗xe7 ♕xe7 3 ♕g4+ ♔h8 4 ♕h4 and if 4 ... f5 to stop 5 ♕xh7 mate, then White simply plays 5 ♕xe7. **5 points**. A standard trick which every player should know. No marks for the immediate 3 ♕h5? when Black can defend with 3 ... f5.

40 1 ♘xg6+ fxg6 2 ♖xh7+ ♔g8 3 ♖xg7+ ♔h8 4 ♖h7+ ♔g8 5 ♖h8 mate or 1 ... ♔g8 2 ♕xc5 ♖ or ♘xc5 3 ♘xe7+ ♔h8 4 ♖xh7 mate. **5 points**. This position could cause a lot of problems, as it is quite easy to forget that White's queen is pinned. Many players might pick up their queen to play 3 ♕xg7 mate only to find out that the move is illegal — it is a mistake even World Champions have been known to make!

Quite a hard set, especially numbers 38 and 40. 20 points maximum for the exercise. *Deduct* 1 point for each minute spent over twelve minutes.

Chapter Three

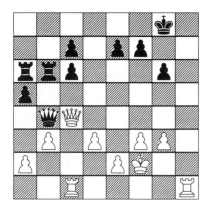

41 Spraggett–Campbell
Canada 1974
White to play and win

42 Rijnbergen–Van Der Tak
Holland 1982
White to play and draw

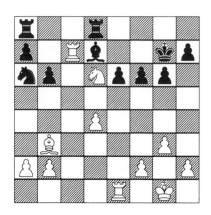

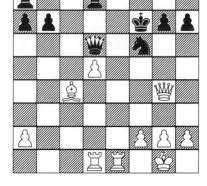

43 Ivanov–Remlinger
USA 1982
White to play and win

44 Bonin–Duric
Philadelphia 1986
White to play and win

Solutions

41　1 ♖h8+! ♔xh8 (1 ... ♔g7 2 ♖h7+) 2 ♕xf7 followed by 3 ♖h1+ wins. **5 points**. Not difficult but easy to miss if you are not familiar with the idea.

42　1 ♘g8! c1=♕+ (or 1 ... ♖xd2 2 ♘f6+ ♔h6 3 ♘g8+ with perpetual check) 2 ♕xc1 ♘d7 (or 2 ... ♕f5 3 ♕c2!! ♕xc2 4 ♘f6+ etc.) 3 ♕f1! ♕e3+ 4 ♔h1 ♕e4+ when it is Black who must take the draw by perpetual. **3 points** for finding 1 ♘g8 and **one additional point** for finding 3 ♕c2 and 3 ♕f1 against Black's different defences.

43　1 ♖xe6! ♘xc7 2 ♖e7+ ♔h6 (2 ... ♔h8 loses to 3 ♘f7+ followed by 4 ♘xd8+ and 5 ♖xd7 while 2 ... ♔f8 allows 3 ♖f7+ ♔g8 4 ♖xd7+ ♔f8 5 ♖f7+! ♔g8 6 ♖xc7+) 3 ♘f7+ ♔h5 (3 ... ♔g7 4 ♘xd8+ and 5 ♖xd7) 4 ♗d1 mate, **5 points**. White is positionally winning anyway, but if you can speed things up with a combination you should do so — provided you are totally confident in your calculations!

44　1 ♖e7+! ♕xe7 (1 ... ♔xe7 2 ♕xg7+ ♔e8 3 ♖e1 +) 2 d6+ ♔e8 3 ♗b5+ ♖d7 (3 ... ♔f7 4 dxe7 +-) 4 dxe7 ♘xg4 and both 5 ♗xd7+ followed by 6 ♗xg4, and 5 ♖xd7 win. **5 points**.

20 points maximum. *Deduct* 1 point for each minute over ten minutes.

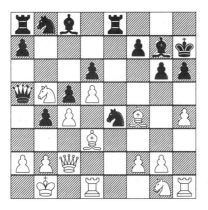

45 Tozer–Agnos
London 1991
Black to play and win

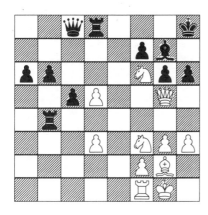

47 Purcin–Riubkin
USSR 1974
White to play and win

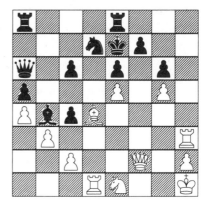

46 Hort–Portisch
Madrid 1973
White to play and win

48 Vladimirov–Haritonov
USSR 1977
White to play and win

Solutions

45 1 ... b3! 2 axb3 (2 ♕xb3 ♘xf2 3 ♘xd6 ♖e1!) 2 ... ♘a6 and White resigned since if 3 ♗xe4 (3 ♘a3 ♘b4 4 ♕c1 ♘xf2 is decisive) 3 ... ♘b4 4 ♕e2 ♕a2+ 5 ♔c1 ♖xe4 wins since 6 ♕xe4 ♕xb2 mates. **5 points**. No heavy sacrifices but still an attractive combination.

46 1 ♖g4+! fxg4 2 ♕g5+ ♔h8 3 ♕h6 wins. On the surface this looks like quite an easy problem to solve but from the black side it is quite easy to overlook that 3 ♕h6 threatens not only 4 ♕xh7 mate but also 4 ♕xf8 mate. **5 points**.

47 1 ♘e5 hxg5 2 ♘xf7 mate or 1 ... ♖f8 2 ♕xg6! ♗xf6 (If 2 ... fxg6 3 ♘xg6 mate) 3 ♕xh6+ ♔g8 4 ♕xf6 wins. **5 points**.

48 1 ♕f6+ ♘xf6 2 ♗c5+! ♗xc5 3 exf6+ ♔f8 4 ♖h8 mate. **10 points**. Short and snappy, but it needs imagination to see it. It is especially hard to see 2 ♗c5+ from the initial position as there are two black pieces guarding that square.

25 points maximum. *Deduct* 1 point for each minute spent over ten minutes.

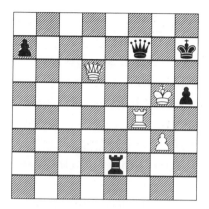

49 **Kiselev–Piskov**
Moscow 1987
Black to play and win

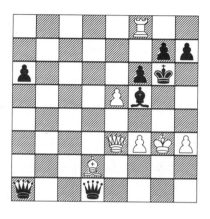

50 **Panfilov–Novochenin**
USSR 1975
White to play and win

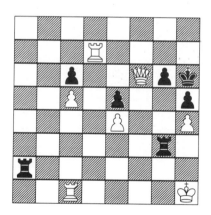

51 **Belyavsky–Christiansen**
Reggio Emilia 1987/88
Black to play and draw

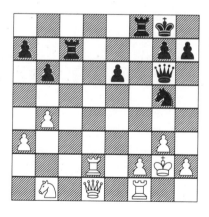

52 **Pigusov–Haritonov**
USSR 1976
Black to play and win

Solutions

49   1 ... ♕g7+ 2 ♔xh5 (2 ♔f5 ♖e5+ 3 ♕xe5 ♕g6 mate) 2 ... ♖h2+ 3 ♖h4 ♖d2 4 ♕e6 (4 ♕xd2 ♕g6 mate) 4 ... ♖d5+ 5 ♕xd5 ♕g6 mate. **5 points**. Seeing 3 ... ♖d2! from the original position is far from easy — although a good chess computer would now solve this type of position in only a few seconds!

50   1 ♕h6+! gxh6 2 ♖xf6+ ♔g7 (2 ... ♔h5 3 ♖xh6 mate) 3 ♗xh6+ ♔g8 4 ♖f8 mate. **5 points**.

51   1 ... ♖h2+! 2 ♔xh2 ♖g2+ 3 ♔h1 ♖g1+ with a draw by perpetual or stalemate. **10 points**. You should have seen the stalemate, but you need to be accurate. Only **5 points** if you chose 1 ... ♖h3+ or 1 ... ♖g1+. Maybe there is still a draw after 1 ... ♖g1+ 2 ♔xg1 ♖g2+ 3 ♔f1 ♖g1+, but it is a long way off.

52   1 ... ♖c1! 2 ♕xc1 ♕e4+ 3 f3 (3 ♔g1 ♘h3 mate) 3 ... ♖xf3 (threatening 4 ... ♖f2+ 5 ♔xf2 ♘h3 mate) 4 ♖xf3 ♕xf3+ 5 ♔g1 ♘h3 mate. **5 points**.

25 points maximum. *Deduct* 1 point for each two minutes over ten minutes.

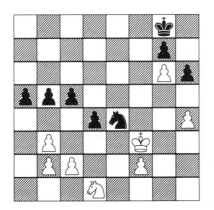

53 Bonner–Medina
Haifa 1976
Black to play and win

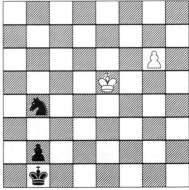

54 Mohr–Conquest
Gausdal 1989
Black to play and win

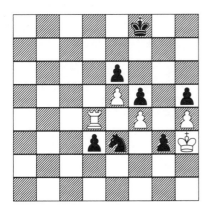

55 Chan–Depasquale
Laoag 1985
Black to play and win

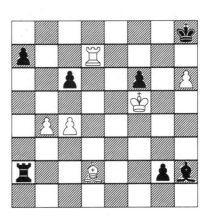

56 Perenyi–Brandics
Hungary 1907
White to play and win

Solutions

53 1 ... ♘c3! 2 bxc3 a4 3 cxd4 cxd4 and the a-pawn touches down. A difficult **5 points**. Knights can be very bad at stopping rooks' pawns.

54 1 ... ♘d5! 2 ♔xd5 (or 2 ♔e6 ♘f4+ and 3 ... ♘xg6) 2 ... ♔c2 (other king moves also win) 3 g7 b1=♕ 4 g8=♕ ♕b3+ wins the queen or 2 g7 ♘e7 3 ♔f6 ♘g8+! 4 ♔f7 ♔c2 and Black queens first and wins. **5 points**.

55 1 ... g2 2 ♔h2 d2 3 ♖xd2 ♘f1+ or 2 ♖xd3 g1=♗! both win. **10 points**, provided you saw the underpromotion, otherwise only **5 points**. Note that after 2 ... g1=♕? White can draw with 3 ♖d8+ ♔e7 4 ♖d7+ and when Black captures the rook White is stalemated. Note also that 2 ... g1=♘+? is no good after 3 ♔h2 ♘f3+ 4 ♔g3.

56 1 ♗g5! g1=♕ (or 1 ... fxg5 2 ♔g6 and 3 ♖d8 mate) 2 ♗xf6+ ♔g8 3 h7+ and wins. **5 points**.

25 points maximum. *Deduct* 1 point for each two minutes over twelve minutes.

Chapter 4

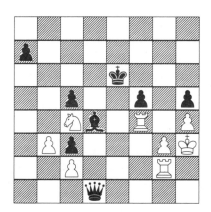

57 Schoch–Littlewood
Winterthur 1986
Black to play and win

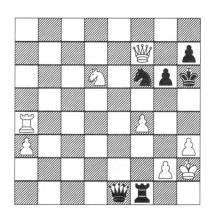

58 Medina–Sanz
Olot 1975
White to play and win

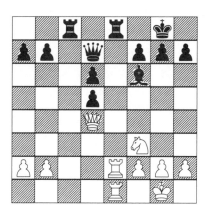

59 Adams–Torre
New Orleans 1920
White to play and win

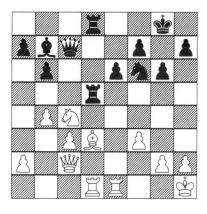

60 Wolf–Rubinstein
Carlsbad 1907
Black to play and win

Solutions

57 1 ... ♗g1 wins as White will have to give up too much material to avoid 2 ... ♕g4+! mating. **5 points**.

58 1 ♘f5+ ♔h5 (1 ... gxf5 2 ♕xf6+ ♔h5 3 ♕g5 mate) 2 ♕xh7+! ♘xh7 3 g4 mate. **5 points**. It is amusing to note that White would be winning even without the rook on a4.

59 1 ♕g4! ♕b5 2 ♕c4! ♕d7 3 ♕c7! ♕b5 4 a4! ♕xa4 5 ♖e4! ♕b5 6 ♕xb7! and Black has no defence. **10 points** in total. **2 points** if you saw as far as 2 ♕c4, **2 points** for each extra move you saw. This problem provides a good example of how deadly the threat of a back rank mate can be.

60 1 ... ♖h5 2 h3 ♘g4! 3 fxg4 ♖xh3+ 4 ♔g1 ♕h2+ and 5 ... ♕xg2+ wins; or 2 ... ♖xh3+ 3 gxh3 ♗xf3+ 4 ♔g1 ♕g3+ 5 ♔f1 ♕xh3+ 6 ♔g1 ♕h1+ 7 ♔f2 ♕g2+ 8 ♔e3 ♘d5+ followed by ... ♘xb4+ decides. **5 points**. From the initial position it is surprising how quickly Black's position crumbles.

25 points maximum. *Deduct* 1 point for each two minutes over fifteen minutes.

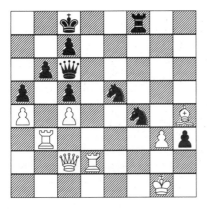

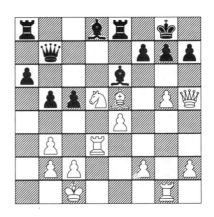

61 Bogoljubow–Monticelli
San Remo 1930
Black to play and win

62 Karasev–Legky
USSR 1978
White to play and win

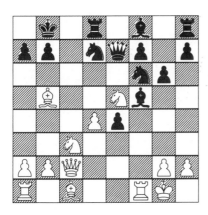

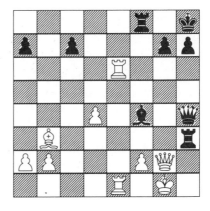

63 Krason–Szypulski
Warsaw 1984
White to play and win

64 Mnatsakanian–Diaz
Varna 1985
Black to play and win

Solutions

61 1 ... ♘e2+ 2 ♖xe2 ♖f1+ 3 ♔xf1 ♕h1+ 4 ♔f2 ♘g4 mate. This problem is deceptively difficult as there are a variety of ways to pursue the attack. **3 points** also for the simple 1 ... ♘f3+ 2 ♖xf3 ♕xf3 3 gxf4 ♕g4+ winning the bishop and with it the game. **5 points**.

62 1 ♕h6 gxh6 2 gxh6+ ♔f8 3 ♗g7+ ♔g8 4 ♗f6+ ♔f8 5 ♖dg3 and mates on g8. **5 points**. Not as easy as it looks. Only **2 points** for 1 ♘f6+ since Black has 1 ... ♗xf6! 2 gxf6 ♕xe4!

63 1 ♘c6+ bxc6 2 ♗f4+ ♔b7 3 ♗xc6+ ♔xc6 4 ♘d5+ ♔xd5 (4 ... ♔b7 5 ♖fc1 wins) 5 ♖ac1 ♘c5 6 ♕c4+ ♔c6 7 ♕a6+ ♔d7 8 ♕b5+ ♔e6 9 ♖xc5 ♘e8 10 ♖e5+ ♔f6 11 ♖xe7 ♔xe7 12 ♕e5 + wins. **5 points** for seeing as far as 2 ... ♔b7 — that is the easy part. How though to follow up? **5 points** extra for seeing as far as 9 ♖xc5, or for choosing instead 3 ♘d5 ♕e6 4 ♘c7.

64 1 ... ♗e3 2 ♖6xe3 (2 fxe3 ♕xe1+; 2 ♖e2 ♗xf2+ 3 ♖xf2 ♖h1+ 4 ♕xh1 ♕xf2 mate; 2 ♕xh3 ♕xf2+ 3 ♔h1 ♕xe1+ 4 ♔h2 ♖f2+ 5 ♔g3 ♕g1+ 6 ♔h4 ♕g5 mate) 2 ... ♖h1+ 3 ♕xh1 ♕xf2 mate. **5 points** if you saw 1 ... ♗e3 and the mating idea with ... ♖h1+.

Definitely getting more difficult. 25 points maximum. *Deduct* 1 point for each 2 minutes over 20 minutes.

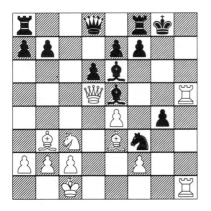

65 Klovsky–Babodzanov
USSR 1978
White to play and win

66 Marciniak–Dobosz
Poland 1973
Black to play and win

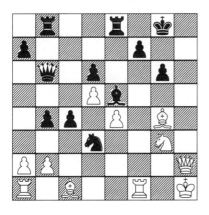
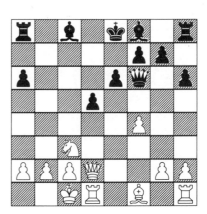

67 Brionnet–Frois
Groningen 1982
White to play and win

68 Braga–Giusti
Sao Paulo 1974
White to play and win

Solutions

65   1 ♖h8+ ♔g7 (1 ... ♗xh8 2 ♕h5 mates) 2 ♖8h7+ ♔g8 3 ♕xe6! fxe6 4 ♗xe6+ ♖f7 5 ♗xf7+ ♔f8 6 ♗h6+ ♗g7 7 ♖xg7 e6 8 ♖h7+ ♔e7 9 ♗h5+ ♔f6 10 ♖f7+ ♔e5 11 ♗g7+, or 7 ... e5 8 ♖h7+ ♔e7 9 ♗h5+ ♔e6 10 ♗g4+ ♔f6 11 ♘d5+ ♔g6 12 ♖g7 mate. There are various ways to win after 1 ♖h8+ ♔g7, e.g. 2 ♖1h7+ ♔g6 3 ♖h6+ ♔g7 4 ♖8h7+ ♔g8 5 ♕xe6 fxe6 6 ♗xe6+ ♖f7 7 ♖xf7. **5 points** if you saw the idea ♖h8+ and ♕xe6.

66   1 ... ♘f2+ 2 ♖xf2 ♗d4! 3 ♕d2 ♗xb2 followed by 4 ... ♗xa1 when Black emerges a rook up. **5 points**.

67   1 ♖xf7 ♔xf7 2 ♕h7+ ♔g7 (2 ... ♔f8 3 ♘f5 and ♗h6 +) 3 ♗h6 ♘f2+ 4 ♔g2 ♕d4 5 ♖f1 wins, as if 5 ... ♖h8 6 ♗xg7 ♖xh7 7 ♗xd4. **10 points**.

68   1 ♘xd5 exd5 2 ♕xd5 ♗a3 3 ♗b5+ axb5 4 ♖he1+ ♗e7 5 ♕d8 mate or 4 ... ♗e6 5 ♕d7 mate. **3 points**. An extra **2 points** if you noticed that Black could avoid immediate loss with 1 ... ♕d8! although the position is still winning for White — gritty defense is an important part of chess!

25 points maximum. *Deduct* 1 point for each two minutes over twenty minutes.

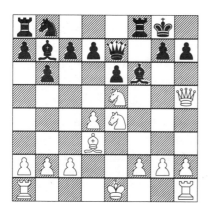

69 Lasker–Thomas
London 1912
White to play and win

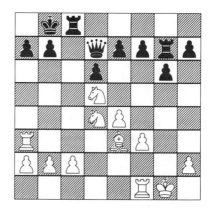

70 Zarcula–Cormos
Yugoslavia 1975
White to play and win

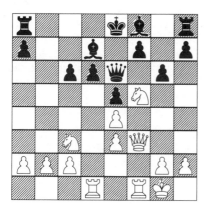

71 Stoica–Larion
Romania 1986
White to play and win

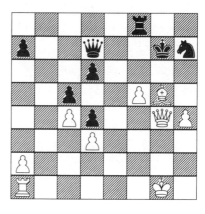

72 Clemens–Wockenfuss
Tresserve 1981
Black to play and win

Solutions

69   1 ♕xh7+! ♔xh7 2 ♘xf6+ ♔h6 (2 … ♔h8 3 ♘g6 mate) 3 ♘5g4+ ♔g5 4 h4+ ♔f4 5 g3+ ♔f3 6 ♗e2+ ♔g2 7 ♖h2+ ♔g1 8 0-0-0 mate. **5 points**. It is not often that you get the chance to castle and mate at the same time!

70   1 ♖xa7! ♔xa7 (1 … ♕d8 2 ♘b5 ♖c6 3 ♘dc7 ♖xc7 4 ♗b6 wins) 2 ♘c6+ ♔a6 (2 … ♔a8 3 ♘b6 mate) 3 ♘cb4+(Ever got the feeling you have seen this idea before!) 3 … ♔b5 (3 … ♔a5 4 ♗b6+ ♔a4 5 b3+ ♔a3 6 ♗e3 ♖xc2 7 ♘xc2+ ♔xa2 8 ♘cb4+ ♔xb3 9 ♖b1+ wins) 4 a4+ ♔xa4 5 b3+ ♔b5 6 c4+ ♖xc4 7 bxc4+ ♔xc4 8 ♘b6+ or 7 … ♔a4 8 ♘b6 or 7 … ♔a5 8 ♖a1 all win). **5 points**. 3 ♘db4+ also wins, e.g. 3 … ♔b5 4 a4+ ♔c4 5 ♘d5 and 6 b3 mate. Pattern recognition is important, but how accurately did you calculate?

71   1 ♖xd6! ♕c4 (1 … ♗xd6 2 ♘g7+ wins the queen) 2 ♘g7+! ♗xg7 (2 … ♔d8 3 ♕f6+ ♔c7 4 ♖fd1 ♖d8 5 ♘e8+) 3 b3 ♕e6 4 ♖xe6+ ♗xe6 5 ♘d5 cxd5 (5 … 0-0 6 ♘c7) 6 exd5 ♗xd5 (6 … ♗f5 7 e4) 7 ♕xd5 0-0 8 ♖xf7 Black resigned. **10 points** if you saw as far as 3 b3, **5 points** for seeing 1 ♖xd6.

72   1 … ♖xf5 (1 … ♕xf5 2 ♗f6+ ♔xf6 3 ♖f1 wins the queen) 2 ♗f4+ ♖g5! is decisive. **5 points**. White's position soon crumbles if he plays quietly, e.g. 2 ♕g3 ♘xg5 3 hxg5 ♕d8 threatening 4 … ♖xg5. Well done if you saw 2 … ♖g5! It is always difficult to consider moving a piece to a square where it is attacked no less than three times.

A bit easier, but still quite a few pitfalls to avoid. *Deduct* 1 point for each minute over fifteen minutes.

Chapter Five

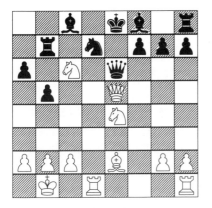

73 Bogda–Ferreira
Paraguay 1976
White to play and win

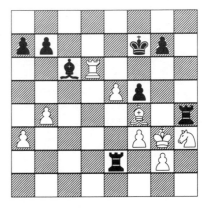

74 Domuls–Terentiev
USSR 1978
White to play and win

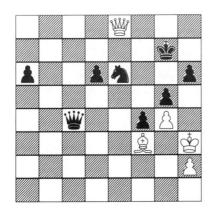

75 Sliwa–Doda
Poland 1971
White to play and draw

76 Sza Lanczi–Herzog
Vienna 1984
Black to play and win

Solutions

73 1 ♘f6+! gxf6 2 ♕xe6+ fxe6 3 ♗h5 mate or ... ♘xf6 2 ♖d8 mate. **5 points**.

74 1 ♖d6 ♖f6 2 ♕c4+ ♔h8 (2 ... ♔f8 3 ♗c5 ♖xd6 4 ♗xd6+ ♔e8 5 ♕g8+ ♔d7 6 ♖d1 wins) 3 ♕xc6! ♖xd6 (3 ... bxc6 4 ♖d8+ mates) 4 ♕xd6 ♕xd6 5 ♘f7+ and wins. **5 points**.

75 1 ♕e7+ ♔g8 (1 ... ♔g6 2 ♗e4+ ♕xe4 3 ♕g7+ ♔xg7=) 2 ♕e8+ ♘f8 3 ♗d5+! ♕xd5 4 ♕xf8+! ♔xf8=. **5 points**. There are of course alternative queen checks at the end. Always be on the look out for a stalemate finish — it can save many a desperate position!

76 1 ... ♖g4+ 2 fxg4 ♖xg2+ 3 ♔h4 ♖xg4+ 4 ♔h5 ♗e8 5 ♗g5 (5 ♖d8 g6+) 5 ... ♔g8+ 6 ♖g6 ♔h7 7 ♘f4 b5! 8 e6 a6 9 e7 ♗f7 10 ♗h4 ♖xf4 11 ♔g5 ♖g4+. **10 points** for seeing as far as the zugzwang with 7 ... b5. **5 points** if you chose 4 ... g6+, although it turns out that White can scrape a draw with 5 ♖xg6 ♖xg6 6 e6+. Quite a hard problem to see right unto the end.

Back to some difficult ones. 25 points maximum. *Deduct* 1 point for each 2 minutes over 20 minutes.

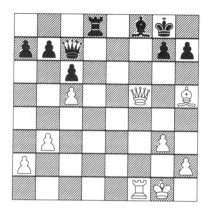

77 Reti–Bogoljubow
New York 1924
White to play and win

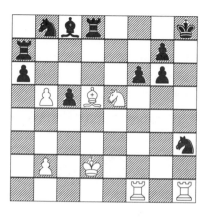

78 Granberg–Gubnicki
Corr 1986
White to play and win

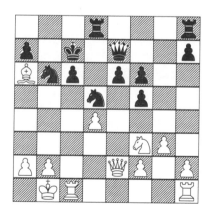

79 Nikitin–Kuznetsov
USSR 1975
White to play and win

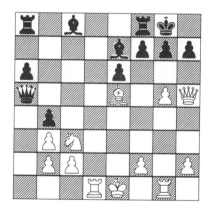

80 Odeyev–Germanavkius
USSR 1988
White to play and win

Solutions

77 1 ♗f7+ ♚h8 2 ♗e8! Black resigned. **5 points.** Harder than it looks.

78 1 ♘d7! ♗xd7 (Any other capture allows 2 ♖xh3 mate.) 2 ♖f3 ♗e6 3 ♖fxh3+ wins. Not 2 ♖f4 ♗e6 3 ♖xh3+ ♚g8 4 ♖fh4 ♖xd5+ and ... ♚f8. **10 points.** A problemist's move!

79 1 ♖xc6+! ♚xc6 (1 ... ♚b8 2 ♖xe6 wins) 2 ♖c1+ ♚d6 (2 ... ♚d7 3 ♗b5+; 2 ... ♘c3 3 ♖xc3+ ♚d6 4 ♕b5 wins) 3 ♕e5+! fxe5 4 dxe5+ ♚d7 5 ♗b5 mate. **3 points** for 1 ♖xc6+ and an additional **2 points** for seeing 3 ♕e5+.

80 1 ♘d5! (Deduct 5 points for the immediate 1 ♕h6?? when Black wins with 1 ... ♕xe5+.) 1 ... exd5 2 ♕h6 threatening 3 ♕xg7 mate and if 3 ... gxh6 4 gxh6+ also mates. **5 points.**

A test of imagination rather than of calculation. 25 points maximum. *Deduct* 1 point for each two minutes over fifteen minutes.

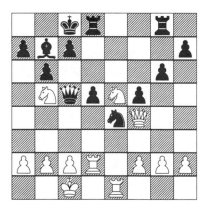

81 Herb–Bellas
France 1978
White to play and win

82 Andruet–Spassky
Koblenz 1988
Black to play and win

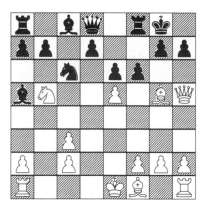

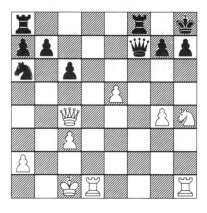

83 Marin–Fernandez
Spain 1981
White to play and win

84 Radovic–Solak
Belgrade 1983
White to play and win

Solutions

81 1 ♘c6! ♖g7 (1 ... ♕xc6 2 ♘xa7+ wins the queen; 1 ... ♖d7 2 ♘bxa7 mate; 1 ... ♘d6 2 ♘bxa7+ ♔d7 3 ♖e7 mate) 2 ♘bxa7+ ♔d7 3 ♕e5 ♗xc6 4 ♕xg7+ ♔d6 5 f3 with the idea 5 ... ♘xd2 6 ♕e7 mate. **5 points** if you saw as far as 3 ♕e5.

82 1 ... ♕f3! 2 gxf3 ♘exf3+ 3 ♔h1 ♗h3 and 4 ... ♗g2 mate. **5 points**. This game was played on Spassky's birthday! Only **1 point** for 1 ... ♗h3 which allows White to fight on with 2 f4!

83 1 ♗d3 h6 2 ♗xf6 ♗xc3+ 3 ♘xc3 ♕a5 4 ♕g6 ♕xc3+ 5 ♔d1 ♖xf6 6 exf6 ♕xa1+ 7 ♔d2 ♕xf6 8 ♕e8+ ♕f8 9 ♗h7+ wins the queen. **10 points**. A hard problem to solve — if you saw the idea with 9 ♗h7+! you have done exceptionally well. Note that 2 ♗xh6 or 2 ♕g6 are both met by 2 ... ♘xe5.

84 1 ♖df1! ♕xc4 2 ♘g6+ ♔g8 3 ♘e7+ ♔h8 4 ♖xh7+ ♔xh7 5 ♖h1 mate. **5 points**. This is an idea worth watching out for.

25 points maximum. *Deduct* 1 point for each two minutes over twenty minutes.

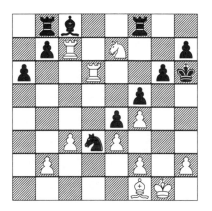

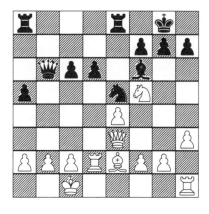

85 Gracs–Radnoti
Hungary 1970
White to play and win

86 Yuferov–Gusev
Kaliningrad 1973
Black to play and win

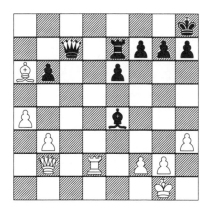

87 Doroshkevich–Federov
USSR 1981
White to play and win

88 Poljes–Kremenetsky
USSR 1973
Black to play and win

Solutions

85   1 ♖f6 ♖xf6 2 ♘g8+ ♚h5 3 ♖xh7+ ♚g4 4 ♗e2 mate or 1 ... ♖d8 2 ♖xc8 ♖bxc8 3 ♘xf5+ ♚h5 4 ♗e2 mate. **5 points**. In the latter line, 2 ♖f7 also wins.

86   1 ... ♗f1 2 ♖xf1 ♕xh2+ 3 ♚e1 ♖c1 mate. **5 points**.

87   1 ♕e5 ♗d5 (not 1 ... ♕xe5? 2 ♖d8+) 2 ♖c2 ♕d7 (If 2 ... ♕xc2 3 ♕b8+ mates) 3 ♖c8+ ♖e8 4 ♕c7! wins. **5 points**.

88   1 ... ♕xb2+! 2 ♚xb2 ♘d3+ 3 ♚a3 (3 ♚b1 ♖ab8 mates; 3 ♚b3 ♖eb8+ 4 ♚c4 ♘b2 mate; 4 ♚a4 ♖b4+ 5 ♚a3 ♗b2 mate) 3 ... ♗b2+ 4 ♚a4 (4 ♚b3 ♖eb8+ 5 ♚c4 ♘e5 mate) 4 ... ♖xe4+! 5 c4 (5 ♕xe4 ♘c5 mate) 5 ... ♖xc4+ 6 ♚b3 ♖c3+ 7 ♚a4 ♖a3 mate. **10 points**. 4 ... ♖xe4+ is the difficult move to find.

25 points maximum. *Deduct* 1 point for each two minutes over twenty minutes.

Chapter Six

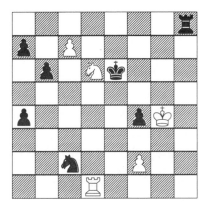

89 Salov–Ehlvest
Sweden 1989
White to play and win

90 Douven–Greenfeld
1988
White to play and win

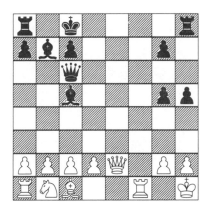

91 Kopeikin–Kulachin
USSR 1973
Black to play and win

92 Speelman–Plaskett
London 1986
White to play and win

Solutions

89 1 ♘e8! (Not 1 c8=♕+ ♖xc8 2 ♘xc8 a3=) 1 ... ♖xe8 2 ♖d8 wins. **5 points.** Quite a hard idea to see.

90 1 ♖c8 ♕b6 (1 ... ♖xc8 2 ♕d8+ mates) 2 ♕d8! wins. **5 points**.

91 1 ... ♖e8 2 ♕f3 ♖e1! 3 ♖xe1 ♕xf3 4 gxf3 ♗xf3 mate. **5 points**. There are other ways of winning on move 2, but this is sharpest. **3 points** for 2 ... ♕xf3 3 gxf3 g4, or 3 ... ♖e1 4 ♔g2 ♗xf3+ 5 ♖xf3 ♖g1+ 6 ♔h3 g4+.

92 1 ♖xb5! ♕xb5 2 ♕b6! ♕a4 3 ♕d8 wins. **10 points**.

A relatively relaxing set. 25 points maximum. *Deduct* 1 point for each minute over twelve minutes.

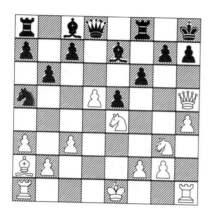

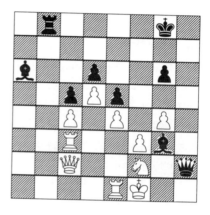

93 **West–Hacche**
Ballarat 1985
White to play and win

94 **Huss–Lobron**
Beer-Sheva 1985
Black to play and win

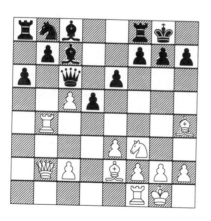

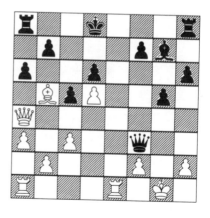

95 **Gachon–St. Denis**
Lyon 1988
White to play and win

96 **Augustin–Lanc**
Brno 1975
White to play and win

Solutions

93 1 d6! cxd6 2 ♘g5 fxg5 3 hxg5 h6 4 ♕xh6+ gxh6 5 ♖xh6+ ♔g7 6 ♘h5 mate. **5 points**.

94 1 ... ♖b3! (threatening 2 ... ♖xc3 3 ♕xc3 ♕f2 mate) 2 ♖e2 (2 ♖xb3 ♗xc4+ and 3 ... ♕xf2 mate) 2 ... ♗xc4 3 ♖xc4 ♖xf3 (threatening 4 ... ♕h1 mate) 4 ♔e1 ♕g1+ 5 ♔d2 ♗f4+ decides. **5 points**.

95 1 ♕xg7+ ♔xg7 2 ♖g4+ ♔h6 3 ♗f6! ♗d8 4 ♗g7+ ♔h5 5 ♖g5+ ♗xg5 6 ♘e5+ ♔h4 7 g3+ ♔h3 8 ♗g4 mate. An even prettier line is 3 ♗g5+ ♔h5 4 ♗f6 (threatening 5 ♖g5+ ♔h6 6 ♗g7 mate) 4 ... ♔xg4 5 ♘h4 mate/5 ♘d4 mate. **10 points** if you calculated either of these lines to mate, **5 points** for seeing as far as either 3 ♗f6 or 3 ♗g5+.

96 1 ♗e8! ♕f5 2 ♖e6! b5 3 ♕a5+ ♔c8 4 ♖e7 and mate on c7. **3 points** for seeing 1 ♗e8 and an extra 2 points for seeing 2 ♖e6 in answer to 1 ... ♕f5.

A slightly easier set. 25 points maximum but *deduct* 1 point for each minute over fifteen minutes.

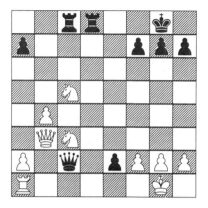

97 Kr. Georgiev–Gulko
St. John 1988
Black to play and win

98 Guseinov–Balajan
USSR 1975
White to play and win

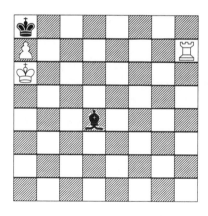

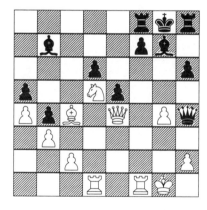

99 Hegde–Palatnik
Calicut 1988
Black to play and draw

100 Romanishin–Poutiainen
Yerevan 1976
White to play and win

Solutions

97 1 ... ♖d1+ 2 ♖xd1 ♕xc3 3 ♕xc3 exd1=♕+ or 3 ♖ moves e1=♕+. **3 points**. An additional **2 points** if you spotted that 1 ... ♕xc3 fails to 2 ♕xc3 ♖d1+ 3 ♕e1 ♖xa1 4 ♕xa1 ♖d8 5 ♕e1 ♖d1 6 ♘d3!! when it is in fact White who wins.

98 1 ♗xh7+ ♔xh7 2 ♖xd8 ♖xd8 3 ♕h5+ ♔g8 4 ♗xg7 ♔xg7 (4 ... ♗xg5+ loses to 5 ♖xg5 ♖d1+ 6 ♔xd1 ♗f3+ 7 ♔c1) 5 ♕h6+ ♔g8 6 g6 wins. **5 points**. This double-bishop sacrifice is well worth remembering as it crops up quite often.

99 1 ... ♗g7 2 ♖h4 ♗d4=. **10 points** if you knew, or worked out that if Black could safely play ... ♗xa7 he is holding the position. **5 points** if you saw the best line but were not sure about the final position.

100 1 ♕g6! ♗xd5 (1 ... fxg6 2 ♘f6 mate; 1 ... ♕g5 2 ♘f6+) 2 ♗xd5 ♕e7 3 ♖xf7 ♖xf7 4 ♖f1 is decisive. **5 points**.

25 points maximum, but *deduct* 1 point for each two minutes over fifteen minutes.

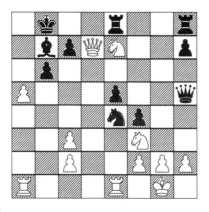

101 Stalfinga–Grahn
Denmark 1974
Black to play and win

102 Vogel–Barlov
West Germany 1981
White to play and win

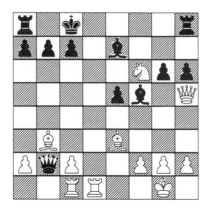

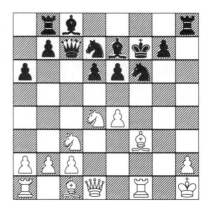

103 Kadrev–Panev
USSR 1972
White to play and win

104 Shulman–Feldmus
USSR 1986
White to play and win

Solutions

101 1 ... ♖xe7! 2 ♕xe7 ♕xf3! 3 gxf3 ♖g8+ 4 ♔f1 ♗a6+ 5 ♖e2 ♘d2+ 6 ♔e1 ♘xf3+ 7 ♔d1 ♖g1+ 8 ♖e1 ♖xe1 mate. **7 points**, plus **3 points** if you saw that 1 ... ♕xf3 is met by 2 ♕xe8+.

102 1 ♗b5! ♖xc6 2 dxc6 ♕c7 (2 ... ♘xe5 3 c7+) 3 cxd7+ ♘xd7 4 ♗xd7+ ♔d8 5 ♗f4 wins. **5 points**.

103 1 ♕xf5+ gxf5 2 ♗e6+ ♔b8 3 ♘d7+ ♔c8 4 ♘c5+ ♔b8 5 ♖b1 ♕xb1 6 ♘a6+ bxa6 7 ♖xb1+ Black resigned. **5 points**. White can also play the moves in a different order e.g. 4 ♖b1, or 5 ♘a6+, or 4 ♘xe5+ followed by ♘c6+.

104 1 ♘xe6 ♔xe6 2 ♕d5+! ♘xd5 3 ♗g4+ ♔e5 4 ♖f5+ ♔d4 5 ♖xd5+ ♔c4 6 ♗e2+ ♔b4 7 a3 mate. **5 points** but only if you saw 2 ♕xd5.

25 points maximum, and *deduct* 1 point for each two minutes over fifteen minutes.

Chapter Seven

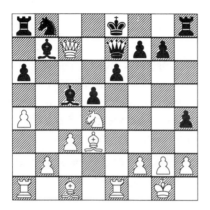

105 Maliskauskas–Oll
Vilnius 1988
White to play and win

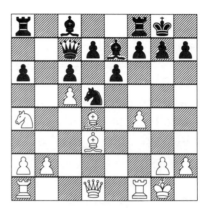

106 Kuzmin–Sveshnikov
USSR Championship 1973
White to play and win

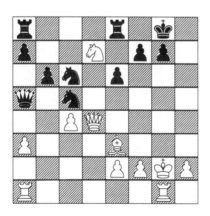

107 Nasonov–Chistiakov
USSR 1978
White to play and win

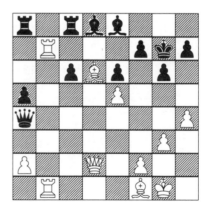

108 Gurevich–Kuzovkin
USSR 1981
White to play and win

Solutions

105 1 ♘xe6 fxe6 2 ♗g6+ ♔f8 3 ♖xe6 ♕xc7 (or 3 ... ♕xe6 4 ♕d8+ mates.) 4 ♖e8 mate. **5 points**.

106 1 ♘b6 ♘xb6 2 ♗xh7+ ♔xh7 3 ♕h5+ ♔g8 4 ♗xg7 ♔xg7 5 ♕g4+ ♔h7 (5 ... ♔f6 6 ♕g5 mate) 6 ♖f3 (threatening ♖h3 mate) 6 ... ♗xc5+ 7 ♔h1 Black resigned. **10 points**. White also has the same combination after the more accurate 1 ... ♖b8 2 ♗xh7+ ♔xh7 3 ♘xd5 cxd5 4 ♕h5+ ♔g8 5 ♗xg7 ♕xc5+ 6 ♔h1 ♔xg7 7 ♕g4+ ♔h8 8 ♖f3 ♕c2 9 f5. Full credit for either line.

107 1 ♘f6+ ♔f8 (1 ... gxf6 2 ♔h1+ ♔f8 3 ♕d6+ ♖e7 4 ♗h6+ wins) 2 ♕d6+ ♘e7 3 ♗h6! ♖ed8 (3 ... gxh6 4 ♔h1 and 5 ♖g8 mate) 4 ♔h1 ♖xd6 5 ♗xg7 mate. **5 points**, **3 points** if you simply intended to snatch material with 3 ♘xe8.

108 1 ♖1b4 axb4 2 ♕h6+ ♔xh6 3 ♗f8+ ♔h5 4 ♗e2 mate. **5 points**; 1 ♖7b4 also works. White must ensure that Black cannot play ... ♕g4 in the final position.

25 points maximum. *Deduct* 1 point for each 2 minutes over fifteen minutes.

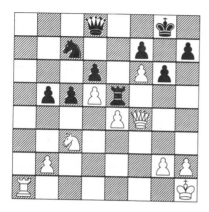

109 Zakharov–Gangiev
USSR 1973
White to play and win

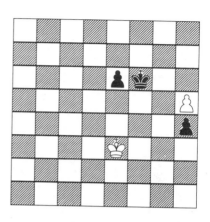

110 Ju. Horvath–S. Horvath
Hungary 1988
White to play and draw

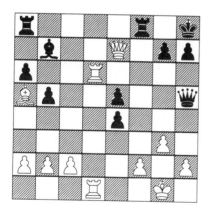

111 Matulovic–Vasyukov
Skopje 1970
Black to play and win

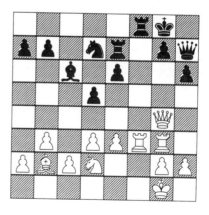

112 Sisniega–Acevedo
Mexico 1976
White to play and win

Solutions

109 1 ♘xb5 g5 (1 ... ♘xb5 2 ♕h6 ♕f8 3 ♖a8! and 4 ♕g7 mate) 2 ♕xe5 dxe5 3 ♘xc7 ♕xf6 4 ♖a8+ ♔g7 5 ♘e8+ wins. **5 points**.

110 1 ♔f4 h3 2 ♔g3 ♔g5 3 ♔h2! ♔h6 4 ♔g3=. The point is that if 3 ... ♔xh5 4 ♔xh3 ♔g5 5 ♔g3 ♔f5 6 ♔f3 ♔e5 7 ♔e3, White keeps the opposition, while if 3 ... e5 4 ♔xh3 ♔xh5 5 ♔g3 ♔g5 6 ♔f3 ♔f5 7 ♔e3, Black is unable to keep the opposition with 7 ... ♔e5. **10 points**.

111 1 ... e3! (Not 1 ... ♖xf2 2 ♖d8+) 2 ♕xb7 (or 2 fxe3 ♕f3 -+) 2 ... exf2+ 3 ♔f1 (3 ♔g2 f1=♕+ 4 ♖xf1 ♕xe2+) 3 ... e4! 4 ♕xe4 ♖ae8 5 ♖d8 (5 g4 ♕h3+ 6 ♕g2 ♖e1+ 7 ♗xe1 fxe1=♕+ 8 ♔xe1 ♕xg2 wins the queen) 5 ... ♖xd8 6 ♖xd8 ♕h3+ 7 ♕g2 ♕xg2+White resigned, since 8 ... f1=♕ follows. A hard-earned **5 points**.

112 1 ♗xg7 ♖xg7 (1 ... ♕xg7 2 ♕h3 wins the queen) 2 ♕xe6+ ♔h8 3 ♕xd7! ♗xd7 4 ♖xf8+ ♖g8 5 ♖fxg8+ ♕xg8 6 ♖xg8+ or 3 ... ♖xf3 4 ♕d8+ ♕g8 5 ♕xg8+ wins. **5 points**.

25 points maximum. *Deduct* 1 point for every two minutes over twenty minutes. Quite a difficult set; in the five-pointers you need to see a fair way ahead to get full credit.

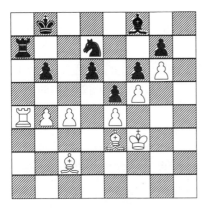

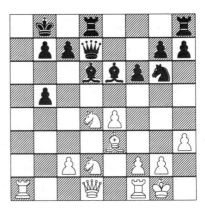

113 Paulic–Vasovic
Yugoslavia 1976
Black to play and draw

114 Wahls–Bjarnason
Malmo 1986
White to play and win

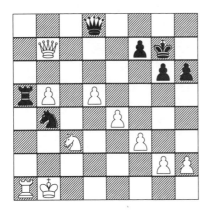

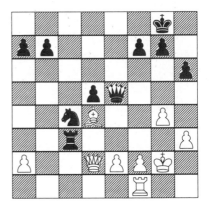

115 Jugasvili–Grigorian
USSR 1976
Black to play and win

116 Letunov–Ubilava
USSR 1973
Black to play and win

Solutions

113 1 ... ♘c5! 2 ♖xa7 ♚xa7 3 dxc5 dxc5 4 ♗a4 ♚b8 5 ♚e2 ♚c7=. **5 points**. A fortress draw. **5 points** also for 1 ... ♖xa4 2 ♗xa4 ♘c5!, or for any quiet move, e.g. 1 ... ♚b7, played in the knowledge that a later ... ♘c5 draws.

114 1 ♖a8+ ♚xa8 2 ♕a1+ ♚b8 3 ♕a7+ ♚xa7 4 ♘c6+ ♚a6 or ♚a8 5 ♖a1+ and mates. **5 points**.

115 1 ... ♕g5 2 ♖xa5 ♕d2 3 ♖a3 (3 ♖a2 ♕d3+) 3 ... ♕c2+ 4 ♚a1 ♘d3 5 ♘a4 ♕d1+ 6 ♚a2 ♘b4+ 7 ♚b2 ♕c2+ 8 ♚a1 ♕c1 mate. **10 points** if you saw the mate. Queen and knight are often a deadly combination.

116 1 ... ♖g3+ 2 ♚h2 (2 fxg3 ♕e4+ and 3 ... ♘xd2 wins) 2 ... ♘xd2 White resigned as if 3 ♗xe5 ♘xf1+ wins. **5 points**. 2 ... ♕c7 also gains full credit.

25 points maximum. A less difficult set, apart from No. 115. *Deduct* 1 point for each two minutes over fifteen minutes.

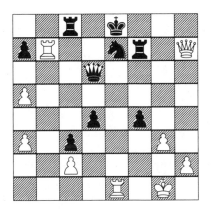

117 Hartston–Whiteley
England 1974
White to play and win

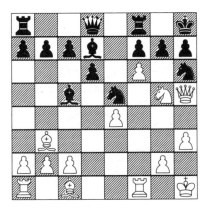

118 Kliefoth–Schliemann
Germany 1862
White to play and win

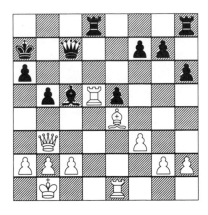

119 Boudre–Pytel
Bagneux 1981
White to play and win

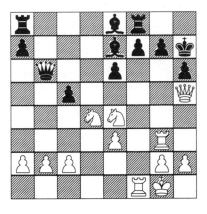

120 Kuijf–Gallego
Andorra 1986
White to play and win

Solutions

117 1 Qg8+ Rf8 2 Qg6+! Qxg6 3 R1xe7+ Kd8 4 Rbd7 mate. **5 points**.

118 1 Nxh7 Kxh7 2 fxg7 Kxg7 3 Qxh6+ Kg8 4 Bg5 and 5 Bf6 wins. **5 points**; the first two moves may be inverted. It is easy to be distracted by the queen sac 1 fxg7+ Kxg7 2 Qxh6+, but there is nothing there!

119 1 Rxc5 Qxc5 2 Qxf7+ Kb6 3 Qb7+ Ka5 4 c3 b4 5 Bd3 Rxd3 6 Rxe5 Rd1+ 7 Kc2 Rd2+ 8 Kxd2 bxc3+ 9 bxc3 Black resigned. **5 points**. At move 5 White has alternatives, notably 5 cxb4+ Qxb4 6 Qc7+ Qb6 7 b4+ Kb5 8 a4+; a similar line also works after 4 a3 instead of 4 c3.

120 1 Rf6! (threatening Rg7+) 1 ... Bxf6 (1 ... cxd4 2 Rxg7+ Kxg7 3 Qxh6+ Kg8 4 Qg5 +; 1 ... gxf6 2 Qg4 mates on g7; 1 ... g6 2 Ng5+ Kg7 3 Ngxe6+ fxe6 4 Rfxg6+! mates) 2 Nxf6+ Kh8 (2 ... gxf6 3 Qg4 again) 3 Qg5! hxg5 (or 3 ... Rg8 4 Qxh6+!) 4 Rh3 mate. **10 points**. Quite snappy for a ten-pointer, but there are a lot of side variations. **8 points** if in the main line you chose a slower win at move 3, e.g. 3 Qg4 g6 4 Qf4 Kg7 5 Qe5.)

25 points maximum. *Deduct* 1 point for each two minutes over fifteen minutes.

Chapter Eight

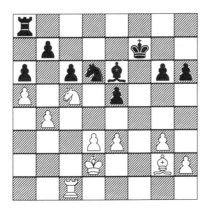

121 Minev–Garcia
Bucharest 1975
White to play and win

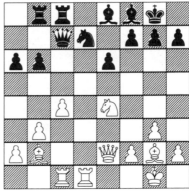

122 Matulovic–Tringov
Siegen 1970
White to play and win

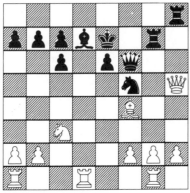

123 Hübner–Vogel
West Germany 1986
White to play and win

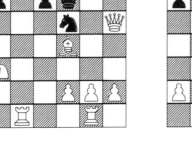

124 Halifman–Aseyev
Borzomi 1984
White to play and win

Solutions

121 1 ♘xb7! ♘xb7 2 ♖xc6 ♖c8 (2 ... ♘xa5 3 ♖c7+; 2 ... ♖d8 3 ♖c7+ ♖d7 4 ♖xb7) 3 ♖xe6 ♔xe6 4 ♗h3+ wins. **5 points**.

122 1 ♘f5 gxf5 2 ♕h4 ♘f8 3 ♕xh5+ ♘h7 4 ♗c5 ♕xc5 5 ♖h3 ♗h6 6 ♕xe8+ ♕f8 7 ♕g6. **5 points**. Some latitude here on the first couple of moves, e.g. 1 ♘xh5 gxh5 2 ♕f5.

123 1 ♘e4! ♖xh5 2 ♖xd7+ ♔xd7 3 ♘xf6+ ♔e7 4 ♘xh5. **10 points**. Some imagination required here.)

124 1 ♖xd7! ♗xd7 (1 ... ♕xd7 2 ♘f6+) 2 ♘f6+ ♔h8 (2 ... gxf6 3 ♕g4+ and 4 ♗xf6) 3 ♕h5 h6 (3 ... gxf6 4 ♗e4!) 4 ♕xf7 Black resigned. **5 points**.

25 points maximum. *Deduct* 1 point for each two minutes over fifteen minutes.

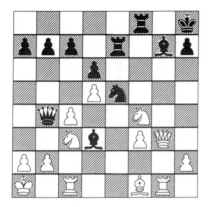

125 Alexandrovic–Borisov
USSR 1974
Black to play and win

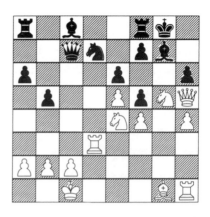

126 Messa–Tonghini
Italy 1984
White to play and win

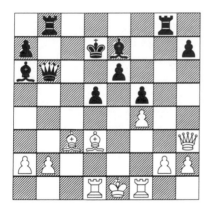

127 Reggio–Mieses
Monte Carlo 1903
Black to play and win

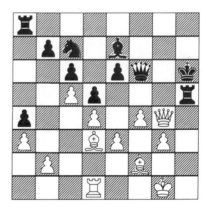

128 Geller–Notaros
Novi Sad 1978
White to play and draw

Solutions

125 1 ... ♖xf4 (Not 2 ... ♘xc4? 3 ♘xd3) 2 ♕xf4 ♘xc4 3 ♖g2 ♗e2! 4 ♖b1 (or 4 ♖c2 ♗xf1) 4 ... ♘a3! 5 ♕f5 (5 ♕c1 ♗xf1 6 ♕xf1 ♗xc3 7 bxc3 ♕xc3+ 8 ♖bb2 ♖e1+) 5 ... ♗f7 wins, since 6 ♕c8+ ♖f8 or 6 ♕e4 ♕xe4. **10 points**. The difficult move is 3 ... ♗e2.

126 1 ♖xd7 ♗xd7 (1 ... ♕xd7 2 ♘f6+ ♗xf6 3 ♕xh6 ♗xg5 4 hxg5 mates on the h-file) 2 ♘f6+ ♔h8 3 ♕xf7! ♖ac8 4 ♕g8+ ♖xg8 5 ♘f7 mate. **5 points**.

127 1 ... ♖g3! 2 ♕xg3 (2 hxg3 ♕e3+) 2 ... ♗h4! 3 ♕xh4 ♕e3+ 4 ♗e2 ♕xe2 mate. **5 points**.

128 1 ♕xh5+ ♔xh5 2 g4+ ♔xg4 (Not 2 ... ♔h6? 3 g5+ +-) 3 ♗e2+ ♔h3 4 ♗f1+ ♔g4 5 ♗e2+ ♔f5 6 ♗d3+ ♔g4 =. **5 points**. A perpetual check more often seen in studies that in games.

25 points maximum. *Deduct* 1 point for each two minutes over twenty minutes.

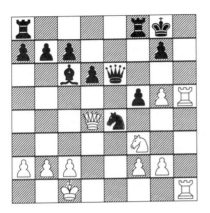

129 Alekhine–Van-Mindeno
Holland 1931
White to play and win

130 Ehlvest–Andersson
Belfort 1988
White to play and win

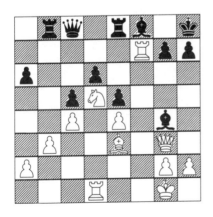

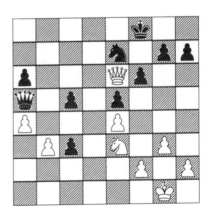

131 Tal–Rantanen
Tallinn 1979
White to play and win

132 Tokarev–Kots
USSR 1973
White to play and win

Solutions

129 1 ♘e5! dxe5 (1 … ♛xe5 2 ♛xe5 dxe5 3 g6 +-) 2 g6 ♛xg6 3 ♛c4+ Black resigned. **5 points.** No points for the immediate 1 g6 which fails to 1 … ♛xg6 2 ♛c4+ d5.

130 1 ♖g8+ ♚xg8 (1 … ♖xg8 2 fxe7+ ♖g7 3 ♖g1 ♛xb2+ 4 ♚d1 ♖cg8 [4 … ♛b1+ 5 ♗c1] 5 e8=♛ or ♖ wins) 2 ♖g1+ ♚h8 3 fxe7+ f6 4 exf8=♛ or ♖+ wins. **5 points**.

131 1 ♘f6! gxf6 (1 … ♗xd1 2 ♛h4 h5 3 ♛g5 ♖b7 4 ♛g6 mates on h7) 2 ♛h4 ♗g7 3 ♗h6 ♗xd1 (3 … ♖g8 4 ♖xd6 ♖b7 5 ♗xg7+ ♖xg7 6 ♖xb7 ♛xb7 7 ♖d8+ ♖g8 8 ♖xg8+ ♚xg8 9 ♛xg4+ wins) 4 ♗xg7+ ♚g8 5 ♗h8! ♚xf7 6 ♛xf6+ finishes Black off. **10 points** in total; **4 points** for the main line, **3 points** for the variation with 3 … ♖g8, 3 points for the variation with 1 … ♗xd1. If you chose the positional 1 ♖df1, then **5 points**; you are probably winning, but you will need good technique. Tal calculates the sacrificial line to its logical conclusion.

132 1 ♘c4 c2 2 ♘d6 c1=♛+ 3 ♚g2 and mate is unavoidable. **5 points**.

25 points maximum. Not too difficult, except for the Tal mind-blower. Even today's World Champion, Garry Kasparov said that Tal was the greatest chess genius that ever lived — I am inclined to agree! *Deduct* 1 point for each two minutes over twenty two minutes.

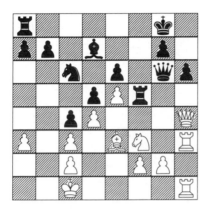

133 Mortensen–Karlsson
Esjberg 1988
Black to play and win

134 **Durkovic–Cserna**
Wolfsberg 1986
White to play and win

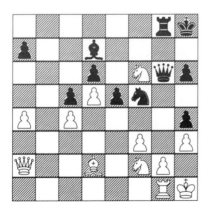

135 Fedder–Westerinen
Roskilde 1978
Black to play and win

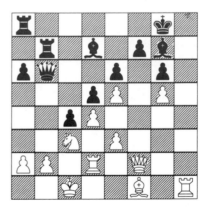

136 **Norwood–Maier**
Groningen 1988
White to play and win

Solutions

133 1 ... ♖xf3 2 ♖xf3 (2 gxf3 ♘b4! 3 ♔d2 [3 axb4 ♗a4 and 4 ... ♕xc2+] ♕xc2+ 4 ♔e1 ♕b1+ 5 ♗c1 [5 ♔e2 ♕d3+] ♕xc1+ 6 ♔e2 ♕xc3 [or 6 ... ♕c2+ 7 ♔f1 ♘d3] 7 ♔f1 ♘d3 wins) 2 ... ♘b4 3 axb4 ♗a4 4 ♔b1 (4 ♔d1 ♕xc2+ 5 ♔e1 ♕d1 mate) 4 ... ♕xc2+ 5 ♔a1 ♗b3 and 6 ... ♕a2 mate. The secret is to notice White's vulnerable c2 square. **5 points**.

134 1 ♖xe6 fxe6 2 ♕h5+ ♔f8 3 ♗h6+ ♔g8 4 ♕xf5! ♘f8 (4 ... exf5 5 ♗c4 mate) 5 ♕g4+ ♔f7 6 ♕g7+ ♔e8 7 ♕xh8+ wins. **10 points**.

135 1 ... ♘g3+ 2 ♔h2 ♘f1+ 3 ♔h1 ♕g3 4 ♘6g4 ♕h2+! 5 ♘xh2 ♘g3 mate. **5 points**.

136 1 ♕f6! ♖ab8 (1 ... ♕d8 2 ♖dh2 and ♖h8+) 2 ♘d1 ♗xf6 3 gxf6 threatening ♖dh2-h8 mate. **5 points**, but no credit for 2 ♖df2 ♗xf6 3 gxf6 ♕xb2+ — I had to include one of Dave Norwood's beautiful wins as he was the best man at my wedding!

A tricky set. 25 points maximum. *Deduct* 1 point for each two minutes over twenty minutes.

Chapter Nine

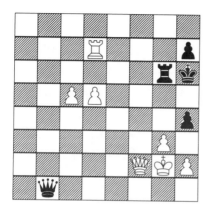

137 Tiberger–Dreshkiewicz
Poland 1970
Black to play and draw

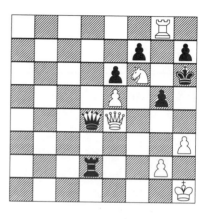

138 Gogolov–Varshavsky
Luksena 1967
Black to play and draw

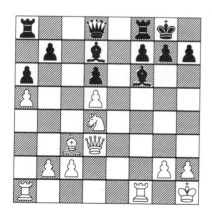

139 Dolmatov–Lautier
Rejkjavik 1988
White to move and win

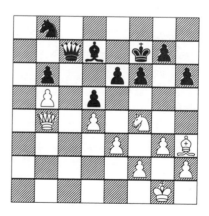

140 Seirawan–Kogan
Philadelphia 1990
White to play and win

Solutions

137 1 ... h3+ 2 ♔xh3 (or 2 ♔f3 ♖f6+) 2 ... ♕f5+ 3 ♕xf5 ♖xg3+ 4 ♔h4 ♖g4+ and after White captures the rook Black is stalemated. **5 points**. Note that 1 ... ♕e4+ loses to 2 ♔g1 ♕b1+ 3 ♕f1.

138 1 ... ♖d1+ 2 ♔h2 ♕g1+ 3 ♔g3 ♖d3+ 4 ♕xd3 (4 ♔g4 ♖d4) 4 ... ♕e3+ 5 ♕xe3 stalemate. **10 points**.

139 1 ♘c6 bxc6 2 ♖xf6 cxd5 (2 ... gxf6 3 ♕g3+ ♔h8 4 ♕g5 wins) 3 ♖xd6 ♕e7 4 ♕d4 f6 5 ♕xd5+ ♖f7 6 ♕xa8+ Black resigned. **5 points** for seeing as far as 2 ♖xf6 and the refutation of 2 ... gxf6.

140 1 ♗xe6+ ♗xe6 2 ♕f8+! ♔xf8 3 ♘xe6+ ♔ anywhere 4 ♘xc7 followed by ♘xd5 with a winning endgame. **5 points**.

An easier set to give the little grey cells a slight rest! 25 points maximum. *Deduct* 1 point for each two minutes over twelve minutes.

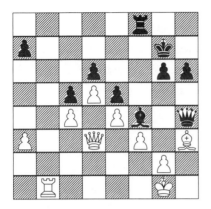

141 **Perez–Benoit**
Nice 1974
Black to play and win

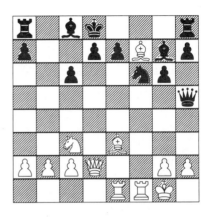

142 **Krystall–Burstow**
Lone Pine 1974
White to play and win

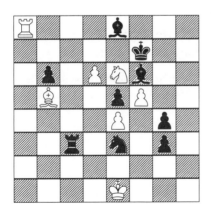

143 **Kouatly–Zapata**
Cap D'Agde 1986
Black to play and win

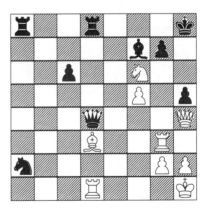

144 **Pasman–Zilber**
Israel 1978
White to play and win

Solutions

141 1 ... Rb8! 2 Kf1 (2 Rxb8 Qe1+ 3 Qf1 Be3+; 2 Rf1 Rb2 3 Qc3 Rxg2+ 4 Bxg2 Bh2+ 5 Kh1 Bg3+ 6 Kg1 Qh2 mate.) 2 ... Be3! and White resigned since he cannot defend against the mate on f2 without losing his rook. **5 points**.

142 1 Rxf6 exf6 (1 ... Bxf6 2 Nd5 and Qa5+) 2 Nd5 cxd5 3 Qa5+ Ke7 4 Bg5+ Kxf7 (4 ... Kd6 5 Qxd5+ Kc7 6 Qc5+ Kb7 6 Bd5+ Ka6 7 Qd6+ wins) 5 Qxd5+ Kf8 6 Qd6+ Kf7 7 Re7+ Kf8 8 Rxd7+ decides. **5 points**. The immediate 1 Nd5, **2 points**, is unclear after 1 ... Nxd5 2 Qa5+ Nc7 3 Bg5 Bd4+ 4 Kh1 d5.

143 1 ... Be7!! (A very hard move to find in a very complicated position. Note that 1 ... Bh4 would lose to 2 Bxe8+ Kf6 3 Bg6! [threatening 4 Rf8 mate] g2+ 4 Ke2! [not 4 Kd2? Be1+! 5 Ke2 Rc2+ 6 Kd3 Rd2+ 7 Kc3 Ra2+ and Rxa8] g1=N+ [or 4 ... Rc2+ 5 Kd3] 5 Kd2 etc.) 2 Bxe8+ (2 Rxe8? g2 3 Rxe7+ Kf6 4 Kf2 Rc1 wins) 2 ... Kf6 3 dxe7 (3 Kd2 g2 4 Ra1 Nf1+ 5 Kxc3 Bxd6 6 Ra7 Be7 wins) 3 ... g2 4 Ba4 g1=Q+ 5 Kd2 Qc1+ 6 Ke2 Qb2+ White resigned. **7 points** for finding 1 ... Be7; a further **3 points** for seeing why the optically good 1 ... Bh4 fails.

144 1 Rxg7 Kxg7 2 Qg5+ Kf8 3 Re1 Be6 (3 ... Qxf6 4 Qxf6 Rxd3 5 Qh8+ Bg8 6 f6 Ra7 7 Qh6+ wins) 4 Qh6+ Kf7 5 Qh7+ Kxf6 (5 ... Kf8 6 fxe6 +-) 6 Rxe6+ Kg5 7 Qg6+ Black resigned. **5 points** for the main line.

25 points maximum. *Deduct* 1 point for each two minutes over twenty five minutes. Suddenly things are getting more difficult!

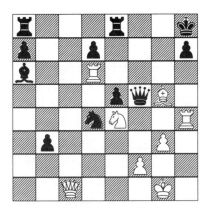

145 Renet–Yudasin
Ostend 1988
White to play and win

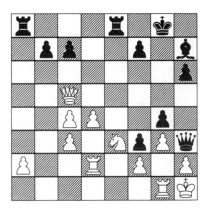

146 Naumov–Petrusanski
USSR 1978
Black to play and win

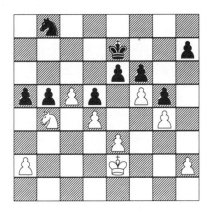

147 Pillsbury–Gunsberg
Hastings 1895
White to play and win

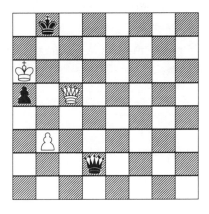

148 Azmaiparashvili–
Ye Jiang Chuan
Beijing 1988
White to play and win

Solutions

145 1 ♖xd4 exd4 2 ♗f6+ ♔g8 3 ♕h6 ♕g6 (3 ... ♖e7 4 ♖h5 and 5 ♖g5+ +-) 4 ♕xg6+ hxg6 5 ♘g5! and Black cannot stop 6 ♖h8 mate. **5 points**.

146 1 ... ♖xe3 2 fxe3 ♗e4! (2 ... f2 is not so good after 3 ♖xf2 ♗e4+ 4 ♖1g2 ♗xg2+ 5 ♖xg2 ♖xa2 6 ♕d5! [not 6 ♖xa2 ♕f1 mate] ♖a1+ 7 ♖g1 ♖a2=) 3 ♖f2 (or 3 ♕e5 f2+ 4 ♕xe4 f1=♕ wins) 3 ... ♖xa2! 4 ♖gf1 ♕xf1+ 5 ♖xf1 f2 mate. **3 points** for 1 ... ♖xe3. And an additional **2 points** if you saw up to 4 ... ♕xf1+.

147 1 c6 ♔d6 (1 ... axb4 2 c7 queens) 2 fxe6 ♘xc6 (2 ... axb4 3 e7 ♔xe7 4 c7 again) 3 ♘xc6 ♔xc6 4 e4! dxe4 5 d5+ ♔d6 6 ♔e3 and the king and pawn endgame is a win by a single tempo: 6 ... b4 7 ♔xe4 a4 8 ♔d4 ♔e7 (Gunsberg chose the weaker 8 ... h5 and lost after 9 gxh5 a3 10 ♔c4 f5 11 h6 f4 12 h7) 9 ♔c4 b3 10 axb3 a3 11 ♔c3 f5 12 gxf5 h5 13 b4 a2 14 ♔b2 a1=♕+ 15 ♔xa1 g4 16 b5 h4 17 b6 g3 18 hxg3 hxg3 19 d6+ ♔xd6 20 b7 ♔c7 21 b8=♕+ ♔xb8 22 e7, queening with check. The last round endgame that Pillsbury needed to win to gain victory in the tournament. **10 points** if you were able to calculate the king and pawn ending to a win; **6 points** if you saw as far as the king and pawn ending.

148 1 ♕c6 (1 ♕xa5? ♕d6+ 2 ♕b6+ ♔a8 3 ♔b5 ♕b4+ draws) 1 ... ♕b4 (1 ... ♕d3+ 2 ♕b5+) 2 ♕d7! threatening ♕d8 or ♕b7 mate. **5 points** — a study-like finish.

25 points maximum. *Deduct* 1 point for each two minutes over twenty five minutes.

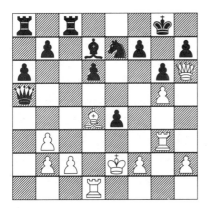

149 Panchenko–Kochiev
USSR 1973
Black to play and win

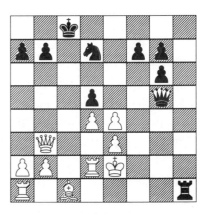

150 Karolyi–Hodgson
Haringey 1989
Black to play and win

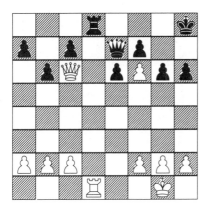

151 Pagilla–Carbone
Argentina 1976
White to play and win

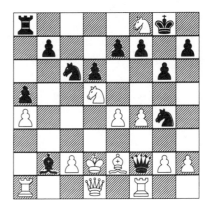

152 Saprikin–Usachev
USSR 1974
Black to play and win

Solutions

149 1 ... ♗g4+! 2 ♖xg4 ♘f5 3 ♕h3 ♖xc2+ 4 ♔f1 ♕b5+ 5 ♔g2 ♕e2 and White resigned. **10 points**. Not immediately 1 ... ♘f5 2 ♕xh7+! ♔xh7 3 ♖h3+ and Black is mated.

150 1 ... ♘c5! (threatening 2 ... ♕g2 mate) 2 dxc5 dxe4 3 ♖d8+ ♕xd8. **5 points**. This game earned me the brilliancy prize — a diamond ring that my wife is now wearing! Note that the immediate 1 ... dxe4 fails to 2 ♕c2+ ♔b8 3 ♕xe4.

151 1 ♕a8 ♖xa8 2 fxe7 and 3 ♖d8 cannot be prevented. Black resigned. **5 points**. Either you see it quickly, or you would never dream of playing it.

152 1 ... ♕d4+ 2 ♗d3 (2 ♔e1 ♗c3+ 3 ♘xc3 ♕xc3+ 4 ♕d2 ♕xa1+) 2 ... ♗c3+ 3 ♔e2 ♕e3+! 4 ♘xe3 ♘d4 mate. **5 points**.

Not a deep set of positions, but pretty. 25 points maximum. *Deduct* 1 point for each two minutes over fifteen minutes.

Chapter Ten

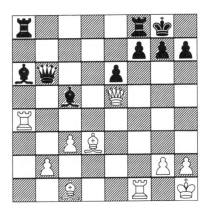

153 Hector–Plachetka
West Germany 1989
White to play and win

154 Vetemaa–Shabalov
USSR 1986
Black to play and win

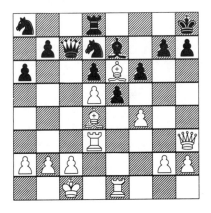
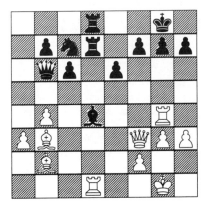

155 Romero Holmes–Cuadras
Torrelavega 1986
White to play and win

156 Meulders–Hartoch
Pieren 1988
White to play and win

Solutions

153 1 ♖g4 f6 (1 … g6 2 ♗h6 f6 3 ♗xg6 fxe5 4 ♗h5+ ♔h8 5 ♗g7+ ♔g8 6 ♗xe5 mate) 2 ♗xh7+ ♔xh7 3 ♕h5+ ♔g8 4 ♖xg7+ ♔xg7 5 ♗h6+ ♔h7 6 ♗xf8+ ♔g8 7 ♖xf6 ♗xf8 8 ♕g6+ ♗g7 9 ♖f7 and Black resigned. **5 points** for this or 1 ♗xh7+ ♔xh7 2 ♖g4. White avoids an incredibly deep trap; 1 ♗xh7+ ♔xh7 2 ♕xg7+ ♔xg7 3 ♖g4+ ♔h8 5 ♖f3 fails to 5 … ♗d3 6 ♖xd3 ♗e3, **5 bonus points** if you saw this. A consolation **3 points** if you actually chose the queen sac; after all, White can still take the perpetual with 5 ♖h3+.)

154 1 … ♕b5! 2 ♖d2 (2 ♗xb5 or 2 ♘xb5 ♘b3 mate) 2 … ♘xc3 3 ♗xb5 ♘b3 mate or 3 bxc3 ♕b1 mate or 3 ♕xc3 ♘b3+ wins. **5 points**.

155 1 ♕xh7+ ♔xh7 2 ♖h3+ ♔g6 3 f5+ ♔g5 4 ♖e4 (4 ♗e3+ ♔g4 5 ♖g3+ ♔h4 6 ♗g5+ fxg5 7 ♖h3+ ♔g4 8 ♖e4 mate also wins.) 4 … exd4 5 ♖g3+ ♔h5 6 ♗f7+ g6 7 ♗xg6+ ♔h6 8 ♖h4+ ♔g7 9 ♗e8+ ♔f8 10 ♖h8 mate. **5 points**. Long but straightforward.

156 1 ♖dxd4 ♖xd4 2 ♕f6! ♘e8 3 ♗xd4 ♘xf6 4 ♗xb6 ♖d3 5 ♖d4!. A nice final touch that simplifies the win. **5 points**.

25 points maximum, and a lot of work for your points! *Deduct* 1 point for each two minutes over twenty five minutes.

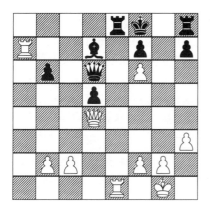

157 Andres–J. Alvarez
Cuba 1988
White to play and win

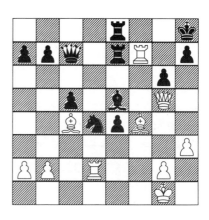

158 Rausis–Gofstein
Sofia 1988
White to play and win

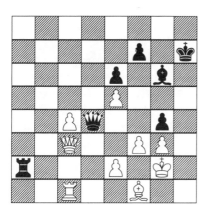

159 Ivanov–Sveshnikov
Chelyabinsk 1973
Black to play and win

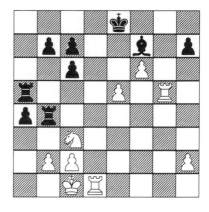

160 Peresipkin–Romanishin
Odessa 1972
White to play and win

Solutions

157 1 ♖e7 ♖d8 (1 ... ♖xe7 2 fxe7+ ♔g8 3 ♖a8+ or 2 ... ♔xe7 3 ♕xh8; 1 ... ♗e6 2 ♖xe8+ ♔xe8 3 ♖a8+) 2 ♖exd7 ♖xd7 3 ♖a8+ ♖d8 4 ♕b4! and 4 ... ♕xb4 is met by 5 ♖xb8 mate. **3 points** for 1 ♖e7 and **2 points** for seeing 4 ♕b4.

158 1 ♗e6! ♘c6 (or 1 ... ♘f5 2 ♗xe5+ ♕xe5 3 ♖xe7 ♖xe7 4 ♖d8+ ♔g7 5 ♖g8 mate) 2 ♖d7 ♖xd7 3 ♖xd7 ♕b8 4 ♖xh7+ ♔xh7 5 ♕h6 mate. **5 points**. A bonus **5 points** if you saw that after 1 ... ♘xe6! 2 ♗xe5+ ♔g8 3 ♕f6 ♕xe5! 4 ♕xe5 ♖xf7 5 ♕xe4 Black can still fight on!

159 1 ... gxf3+ 2 ♔xf3 ♖a3! 3 ♕xa3 ♗e4+ 4 ♔g4 ♗g2+ 5 ♔g5 ♕xe5+ 6 ♔h4 ♕f6+ 7 ♔g4 ♕f5+ 8 ♔h4 ♕h3+ 9 ♔g5 ♕h6+ 10 ♔g4 f5 mate. **10 points**. A long but reasonably straightforward variation to calculate.

160 1 e6 ♖xg5 2 ♖d8+! ♔xd8 3 exf7 and the pawn queens. **5 points**.

25 points maximum. My apologies if No. 158 was slightly misleading. *Deduct* 1 point for each two minutes over twenty minutes.

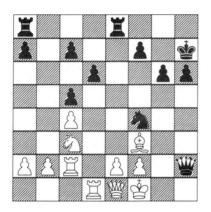

161 **Friedman–Thornblom**
1973-74
Black to play and win

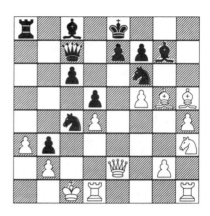

162 **Sax–Kestler**
Nice 1974
Black to play and win

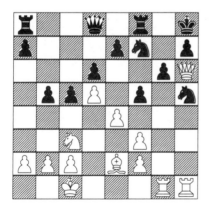

163 **Planinc–Marangunic**
Novi Travnik 1969
White to play and win

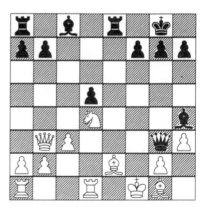

164 **Persowski–Sobura**
Poland 1985
Black to play and win

Solutions

161 1 ... ♖e3! 2 fxe3 ♘h3 and 3 ... ♕g1 mate. **5 points.** No points for the immediate 1 ... ♘h3 which allows White's king to escape with 2 e3!

162 1 ... ♖xa3! 2 bxa3 (2 ♔b1 ♖a1+ 3 ♔xa1 ♕a5+ followed by ... ♕a2+ and ... ♕a1 mate) 2 ... ♕a5 3 ♖d3 (3 ♖he1 ♕c3+; 3 ♖de1 ♕c3+ 4 ♔d1 ♕a1 mate) 3 ... ♕xa3+ 4 ♔b1 ♗xf5 5 ♘f2 b2 6 ♗xf7+ (6 g4 ♕b3) ♔xf7 7 ♗xf6 ♕a1+ 8 ♔c2 b1=♕+ 9 ♖xb1 ♕a2+ White resigned. **5 points** for seeing as far as 5 ... b2.

163 1 ♕xg6 hxg6 2 ♖xg6 ♘h6 3 ♖xh5 ♖f7 3 ♖gxh6+ ♔g7 4 ♖h7+ ♔g8 (4 ... ♔f6 5 ♖5h6+ ♔g5 6 f4+) 5 ♖h8+ ♔g7 6 ♖5h7+ ♔g6 7 exf5+ ♖xf5 8 ♖xd8 ♖xd8 ♗d3 ♔xh7 10 ♗xf5+ ♔g7 11 ♘xb5 ♔f6 12 ♗g4 Black resigned. **10 points** for seeing as far as 9 ♗d3. **6 points** for seeing as far as the sequences of checks on the h-file.

164 1 ... ♖xe2! 2 ♔xe2 (2 ♘xe2 ♕xf3+ 3 gxf3 ♗h3 mate) 2 ... ♕xg2+ 3 ♗f2 (3 ♔e3 ♗g5+ 4 ♔d3 ♕e4 mate; 3 ♔d3 ♕e4+ 4 ♔d2 ♗g5+ 5 ♖e3 ♗xe3+ 6 ♔e2 ♗xd4+ wins) 3 ... ♕xf2+ 4 ♔d3 ♗f5+ 5 ♘xf5 ♕xf5+ 6 ♔d2 ♗g5+ 7 ♔e1 ♖e8 mate. **5 points** for seeing as far as 3 ... ♕xf2+, by which time it is clear that Black is winning. Of course, you had to see the queen sac.

25 points maximum. *Deduct* 1 point for each two minutes over twenty minutes. An exercise in accurately seeing an attack through.

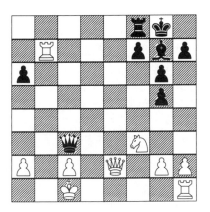

165 Ermenkov–West
Miskolc/Tapolca 1990
Black to play and win

166 Srinivas–Ravi Kumar
India 1984
Black to play and win

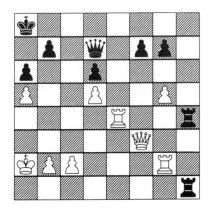

167 Tisdall–J. Polgar
Reykjavik 1988
Black to play and win

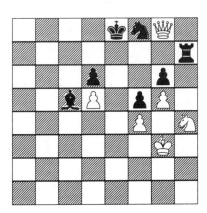

168 Ree–Hort
Wijk aan Zee 1986
Black to play and draw

Solutions

165 1 ... Qa1+ 2 Rb1 Bb2+ 3 Kd2 Rd8+ 4 Nd4 (4 Ke3 Bd4+ 5 Nxd4 Qxd4+ 6 Kf3 Qf4 mate) 4 ... Rxd4+ 5 Ke3 Qxa2 (threatening 6 ... Re4+ 7 Kxe4 Qe6+ 8 Kd3 Qd5+ 9 Ke3 Qd4+ 10 Kf3 Qf4 mate) 6 Kf2 (6 g3 Qe6+ 7 Kf2 Qf5+ 8 Kg2 Qd5+ 9 Kg1 Rd2 10 Qe8+ Kg7 and wins) 6 ... Rf4+ 7 Kg3 Qa3+ 8 Qd3 Bd4! 9 Kh3 (9 Qxa3 Bf2+ 10 Kh3 Rh4 mate) 9 ... g4+ 10 Kh4 (or 10 Kg3 Qd6) Qe7+ 11 Kg3 Bf2+ 12 Kxf4 Qf6+ 13 Kxg4 (or 13 Ke4 Qf5 mate) 13 ... h5+ 14 Kh3 Qh4 mate. **10 points** for seeing the main line as far as 8 ... Bd4.

166 1 ... Nd4! 2 cxd4 Bg4 3 Qxb7 Rab8 4 Qxa7 Qxb1+! and 5 ... Bb4 mate. **5 points**.

167 1 ... R1h3 2 Qe2 Qa4+ 3 Rxa4 Rxa4+ 4 Kb1 Rh1+ mates. **5 points.** What odds on Judit Polgar becoming the first woman to be Champion of the World?

168 1 ... Rxh4 2 Kxh4 Bd4! draws. **5 points.** A remarkable idea. Black simply plays his king to e7 and oscillates his bishop along the a1-h8 diagonal, when White can make no progress. I was actually present when Hort played this game — the smile on his face afterwards is something I shall never forget — drawing can be even more satisfying than winning sometimes.

25 points maximum. *Deduct* 1 point for each two minutes over twenty minutes.

Chapter Eleven

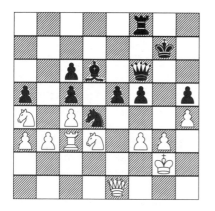

169 Vaganian–Balashov
Vilnius 1975
Black to play and win

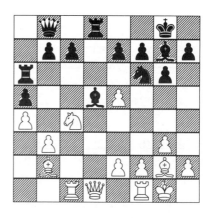

170 Pigusov–Malaniuk
USSR 1978
White to play and win

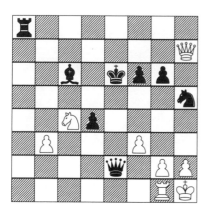

171 Buza–Vaisman
Mongolia 1977
Black to play and win

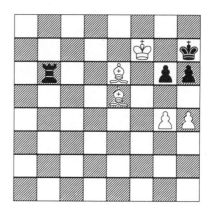

172 Smyslov–Blackstock
London 1988
Black to play and draw

Solutions

169 1 ... e4 2 fxe4 Nf3! 3 Qe3 (3 Kxf3 fxe4+ 4 Ke2 Qf3+ 5 Kd2 exd3 6 Rxd3 Qg2+ 7 Kc3 Rf1 wins) 3 ... fxe4 4 Qxe4 (4 Nf2 Bxg3 5 Nxe4 [or 5 Kxg3 Qxh4+ 6 Kg2 Qh2+ 7 Kf1 Qg1+ 8 Ke2 Qe1 mate] Qxh4 wins.) 4 ... Nxh4+ 5 Qxh4 Qf1+ 6 Kh2 Qe2+ 7 Kh3 Be7 8 Qf4 Rxf4 9 Nxf4 Qd1 10 Kg2 Bd6 11 Nd3 Qe2+ 12 Nf2 Be5 13 Rf3 Bd4 14 Nc3 Qb2 wins. **10 points** for seeing as far as 7 ... Be7. **5 points** for seeing as far as 2 ... Nf3.

170 1 exf6 Bxg2 2 fxe7 Rxd1 3 Rfxd1 Qe8 4 Rd8 Bc6 (or 4 ... Ra8 5 Rcd1 threatening 6 Rxa8.) 5 Nd6! cxd6 6 Rxc6 Ra8 7 Rxa8 Qxa8 8 Rxd6 threatening 9 Rd8, and Black resigned. **5 points**; **3 points** if you only saw as far as 4 Rd8.

171 1 ... Bxf3 2 Qxg6 Qxg2+ 3 Qxg2 (or 3 Rxg2 Ra1 mate) 3 ... Ng3+ 4 hxg3 Rh8 mate. **5 points**. But not 1 ... Qxf3? 2 Re1+.

172 1 ... h5! 2 gxh5 (2 g5 Rb7+ 3 Kf8 Rf7+ 4 Ke8 Re7+ draws) 2 ... Rb7+ (not 2 ... gxh5 3 Bf5+ Kh6 4 Bg7 mate) 3 Kf6 gxh5 4 Kg5 Rg7+ 5 Kxh5 Rg5+! forces stalemate. **5 points**. If 4 Bf5+ Kg8 5 Kg5 Rb5 draws. Also, after 4 Kg5, ... Rb5 is OK.

25 points maximum. *Deduct* 1 point for each two minutes over twenty minutes.

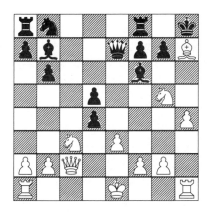

173 Arebo–Spielke
Corr 1973
White to play and win

174 Grigoriev–Nadiseva
USSR 1973
Black to play and win

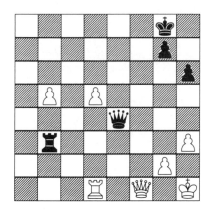

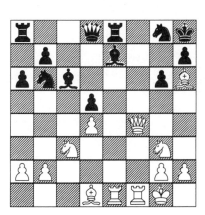

175 Gipslis–K. Urban
Berlin 1991
White to play and win

176 Glek–Ivanenko
USSR 1986
White to play and win

Solutions

173 1 ♗g6! (1 ♗g8 fails to 1 ... g6) 1 ... fxg6 (1 ... dxe3 2 ♗xf7 exf2+ 3 ♔d2; 1 ... ♗a6 2 ♗xf7 d3 3 ♕d1 g6 4 h5 ♗xg5 5 hxg6+ ♔g7 6 ♖h7+ ♔f6 7 ♕f3+ ♔e5 8 ♕xd5+ ♔f6 9 ♕d4+ ♕e5 10 ♘d5+ ♔f5 11 g4 mate.) 2 ♕xg6 ♗xg5 3 hxg5+ ♔g8 4 ♖h8+ ♔xh8 5 ♕h5+ ♔g8 6 g6 Black resigned. **10 points**. No need to calculate the 1 ... ♗a6 line beyond 3 ♕d1.

174 1 ... ♕d2 2 ♖xb3 ♕c1+ 3 ♔xa2 ♖xa3+ and White resigned as 4 ♔xa3 or 4 bxa3 ♕a1 is mate or 4 ♖xa3 ♕xb2 mates. **5 points**.

175 1 d6 ♖xh3+ 2 ♔g1 ♕e3+ 3 ♕f2 ♖h1+ 4 ♔xh1 ♕xf2 5 d7 ♕h4+ 6 ♔g1 ♕d8 7 ♖d4 (So as to play b6 without allowing the queen to capture with check) 7 ... ♔f7 8 b6 ♔e6 9 b7 ♔e7 10 ♔h1 (10 ♖e4+ is more direct) 10 ... h5 11 ♖e4+ ♔f7 (11 ... ♔xd7 12 ♖d4+; 11 ... ♔d6 12 ♖b4 ♕b8 13 d8 = ♕+) 12 ♖b4 Black resigned. **5 points**. Passed pawns must be pushed! Only **2 points** for 1 ♔g1 ♕e3+ 2 ♕f2 ♕xf2+ 3 ♔xf2 ♖xb5 4 d6 ♖b8; the endgame is not to be won. Many White players might well stop their analysis when they see 3 ... ♖h1+ — well done, if you continued your's.

176 1 ♘h5 gxh5 (1 ... ♘xh6 2 ♕xh6 ♖g8 3 ♖f7 and mates on h7) 2 ♗g7+ ♔xg7 3 ♕f7+ ♔h8 4 ♗c2 and mates on h7. **5 points**. Not 1 ♗g7+ ♔xg7 2 ♕f7+ ♔h8 3 ♘h5 ♗f8.

25 points maximum. *Deduct* 1 point for each two minutes over twenty minutes.

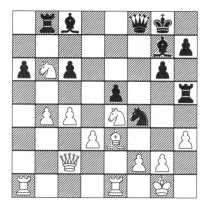

177 Filguth–Remon
Bayamo 1986
Black to play and win

178 **Vilela–Granda Zuniga**
Bayamo 1986
Black to play and win

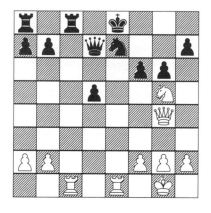

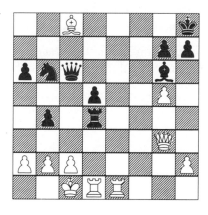

179 Steinitz–Von Bardeleben
Hastings 1895
White to play and win

180 **Halifman–Ehlvest**
USSR 1985
White to play and win

Solutions

177 1 ... ♘xg2! 2 ♔xg2 (or 2 ♘xc8 ♘xe1) 2 ... ♗xh3+ 3 ♔g3 (or 3 ♔g1 ♕f3 mating) 3 ... ♗g4 4 ♘d2 (4 ♔xg4 ♕f5+ 5 ♔g3 ♖h3+ 6 ♔g2 ♕f3+ 7 ♔g1 ♖h1 mate) 4 ... ♖h3+ 5 ♔g2 ♗f3+ 6 ♔xh3 ♕f5+ 7 ♔h2 ♕h5+ 8 ♔g3 ♕g4+ 9 ♔h2 ♕g2 mate. **5 points**. Long but straightforward.

178 1 ... ♘h3+ 2 gxh3 (2 ♔h1 ♘xf2+ 3 ♔g1 ♘xd1 4 ♘xf6 ♘xe3; 2 ♔f1 ♖xf2+ 3 ♔e1 ♘d3+) 2 ... ♖g8+ 3 ♔f1 (3 ♔h1 ♘e4) 3 ... ♗a6+ 4 ♔e1 ♘e4 5 ♖c8 ♗xc8 6 ♘xf6 ♖g1+ 7 ♔e2 ♗a6+ 8 ♔f3 ♘g5+ 9 ♔f4 ♘xh3+ 10 ♔f5 ♖xd1 White resigned. **6 points** for seeing as far as 4 ... ♘e4; the full **10 points** only if you saw the defensive resource 5 ♖c8 and its refutation.

179 1 ♖xe7+! ♔f8 (1 ... ♔xe7 2 ♖e1+ ♔d6 [2 ... ♔d8 3 ♘e6+] 3 ♕b4+ ♖c5 4 ♖e6+ wins) 2 ♖f7+ ♔g8 3 ♖g7+ ♔h8 (3 ... ♔f8 4 ♘xh7+) 4 ♖xh7+ ♔g8 5 ♖g7+ ♔h8 6 ♕h4+ ♔xg7 7 ♕h7+ ♔f8 8 ♕h8+ ♔e7 9 ♕g7+ ♔e8 10 ♕g8+ ♔e7 11 ♕f7+ ♔d8 12 ♕f8+ ♕e8 13 ♘f7+ ♔d7 14 ♕d6 mate. **5 points**. Not a ten-pointer as many of you will have seen this position before. Still, it is useful practice to try to think through these classic combinations for yourself.

180 1 ♗f5 ♗xf5 2 ♕c7! ♖xd1+ 3 ♔xd1 ♗xc2+ 4 ♔c1 ♗a4+ 5 ♕xc6 ♗xc6 6 ♖e6 Black resigned. **5 points**. Fast play along open lines. Did Black think he was winning?

25 points maximum. *Deduct* 1 point for each two minutes over twenty five minutes. Some long variations to be calculated in this exercise.

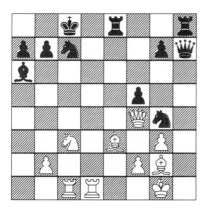

181 Alexandrov–Zakev
USSR 1973
White to play and win

182 Chernin–Aseyev
USSR 1978
White to play and win

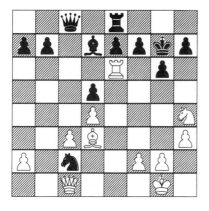

183 Popov–Smuter
USSR 1988
White to play and win

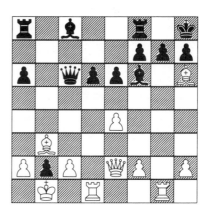

184 Rufenacht–Mattheus
Thessaloniki 1984
White to play and win

Solutions

181 1 ♕xc7+! ♔xc7 2 ♘b5+ ♔b8 3 ♖d8+ (Not 3 ♗f4+ ♖e5!) 3 … ♖xd8 4 ♗f4+ ♔a8 5 ♘c7+ ♔b8 6 ♘xa6+ ♔a8 7 ♘c7+ ♔b8 8 ♘d5+ ♔a8 9 ♘b6+ axb6 10 ♖a1 mate. A real brilliancy. **10 points** if you saw it through.

182 1 ♗g5 (threatening 2 ♗xf6+ ♔xf6 3 ♕xe5+) 1 … ♘xe6 (1 … fxg5 2 ♕xe5+ ♔h6 3 ♘f7+) 2 ♗xf6+ ♔g8 3 dxe6 ♖xd6 4 ♕xe5 b5 5 ♗h8 ♕b7 6 e7 ♔f7 7 e8 = ♕+ Black resigned. **5 points** for seeing as far as 4 ♕xe5.

183 1 ♕h6+ ♔xh6! (1 … ♔g8 2 ♘f5 gxf5 3 ♗xf5 or 1 … ♔h8 2 ♘xg6+ fxg6 3 ♗xg6 wins) 2 ♘f5+ ♔h5 (2 … ♔g5 3 h4+ ♔f4 [3 … ♔g4 4 f3+ ♔f4 5 ♔f2 and 6 g3 mate] 4 g3+ ♔g4 5 f3+) 3 f4 gxf5 4 ♗e2+ ♔h4 5 ♔h2 and 6 g3 or 6 ♖h6 mate. **5 points** for calculating 1 … ♔xh6 to a mate.

184 1 e5! dxe5 (1 … ♗xe5 2 ♕xe5!; 1 … gxh6 2 exf6 ♗b7 3 ♕h5 ♕f3 4 ♕xh6 ♖g8 5 ♔xb2 wins) 2 ♗xg7+ ♗xg7 3 ♖xg7 ♔xg7 4 ♕g4+ ♔f6 5 ♕h4+ ♔f5 6 ♕xh7+ ♔f4 7 ♕h4+ ♔f5 8 ♖g1 Black resigned. **5 points**.

25 points maximum. *Deduct* 1 point for each two minutes over twenty minutes.

Chapter Twelve

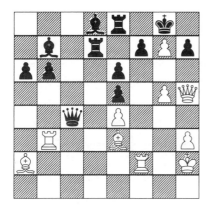

185 Gross–Hort
Czechoslovakia 1975
White to play and win

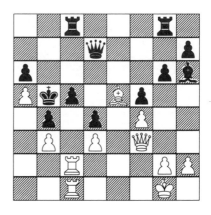

186 Smirnov–Rotstein
USSR 1976
White to play and win

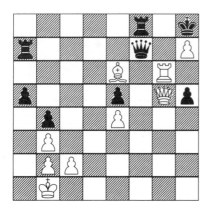

187 Yudasin–Kovalev
Simferopol 1988
Black to play and draw

188 Tarrasch–Grünfeld
Naples 1914
White to play and win

Solutions

185 1 ♖d3! ♕c6 (1 ... ♕xd3 2 g6 fxg6 3 ♗xe6+ ♖xe6 4 ♖f8+ ♔xg7 5 ♗h6 mate; 1 ... ♕xe4 2 ♖xd7 ♕h1+ 3 ♔g3 wins) 2 ♖xd7 ♕xd7 3 g6 fxg6 4 ♖f8+ ♖xf8 5 ♕xh7+ ♔xh7 6 gxf8=♘+ ♔g7 7 ♘xd7 b5 (7 ... ♗xe4 8 ♘xb6) 8 ♘c5 ♗c8 9 ♗xe6 wins. **10 points** for seeing up to 6 gxf8=♘+; **5 points** for finding 1 ♖d3.

186 1 ♘b6! ♘xb6 2 ♖c7 ♕xc7 (2 ... h5 3 ♕h3; 2 ... ♕e8 3 ♕xe6+ ♔h8 4 ♖xe7 ♕xe7 5 ♗b2+ ♔g7 6 ♘f7+ ♔g8 7 ♘h6+ ♔h8 8 ♕g8 mate) 3 ♕xe6+ ♔g7 (3 ... ♔h8 4 ♗b2+ ♗g7 5 ♘f7+ ♔g8 6 ♘h6+ ♔h8 7 ♕g8+ mates) 4 ♗b2+ ♔h6 5 ♕h3+ (5 ♘f7+ ♔h5 6 ♕h3 mate) 5 ... ♔xg5 6 f4 mate. **5 points** for main line.

187 1 ... ♕xg6 2 ♕xg6 ♖g7 3 ♕xh5 ♖g1+ 4 ♔a2 ♖ff1 5 ♕xe5+ ♔xh7 draws. **5 points**. White has no constructive checking sequence in the final position.

188 1 ♗c7! ♖xc7 (1 ... ♕xc7 2 ♖xc5+ ♕xc5 3 ♕b7+) 2 ♕b7+ ♖xb7 3 ♖xc5 mate. **5 points**. A problem theme.

25 points maximum. *Deduct* 1 point for each two minutes over twenty minutes.

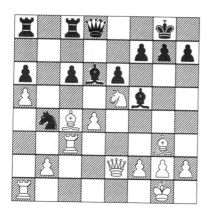

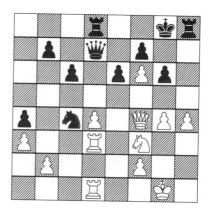

189 Lederman–Eperjesi
Biel 1981
White to play and win

190 Johansen–
　　　　Gedevanishvili
Sydney 1989
White to play and win

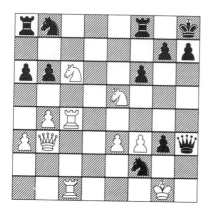

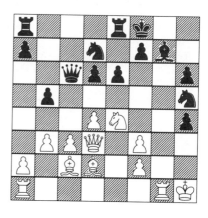

191 Mestel–Gufeld
Hastings 1987
White to play and win

192 Hoi–Gulko
Thessaloniki 1988
White to play and win

Solutions

189 1 ♘xf7! ♔xf7 2 ♗xe6+ ♗xe6 3 ♖f3+ ♔e7 (3 … ♔g8 4 ♕xe6+ ♔h8 5 ♗xd6 ♘c2 6 ♖d1 ♕xa5 7 ♗e5 wins) 4 ♖e1 ♕g8 (4 … ♕d7 5 ♗h4+) 5 ♖e3 ♗xg3 6 ♖xe6+ ♔d7 7 ♖e7+ ♔d6 8 ♖d7+ ♔xd7 9 ♕e7 mate. **5 points**.

190 1 d5! ♘xb2 (1 … cxd5 2 ♕xc4 wins a piece) 2 ♖3d2 (2 dxe6 ♘xd3) 2 … ♘xd1 3 dxe6 ♕c8 4 ♖xd8+ ♕xd8 5 e7 ♕e8 6 ♕d2. Now 6 … ♔h7 7 ♘g5+ wins so Black resigned. **5 points**.

191 1 ♖h4! ♕xh4 2 ♕g8+ ♔xg8 (2 … ♖xg8 3 ♘f7 mate) 3 ♘e7+ ♔h8 4 ♘f7+ ♖xf7 5 ♖c8+ mates. **5 points**. A stunning "one-liner".

192 1 ♖xg7 ♔xg7 (1 … ♘xg7 2 ♗xh6 followed by ♖g1 wins) 2 ♗xh6+ ♔xh6 3 ♖g1 f5 (3 … ♘f4 4 ♘g5 ♘xd3 5 ♘xf7+ ♔h7 6 ♗xd3+ mates and 4 … f5 5 ♕e3 wins) 4 ♕e3+ f4 (4 … ♔h7 5 ♕g5) 5 ♘xd6 ♕xd6 (5 … fxe3 6 ♘f7 mate; 5 … ♘g3+ 6 ♖xg3 fxe3 7 ♘f7+ ♔h5 8 ♖g5 mate) 6 ♕d3 ♘g3+ (6 … ♘f8 7 ♕h7+) 7 ♖xg3 ♘f8 8 ♖g6+ ♔h5 9 ♖f6 ♕e7 10 ♖xf8 ♕g7 11 ♖xf4 with the winning ♖g4 to follow. **10 points**. Some heavy sacrifices, so the lines have to be calculated a long way.

25 points maximum. *Deduct* 1 point for each two minutes over thirty minutes.

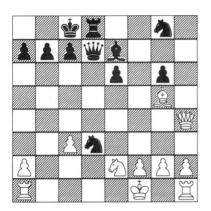

193 Janovsky–Muratov
USSR 1988
Black to play and win

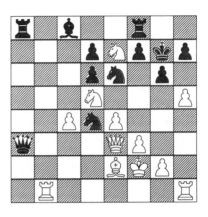

194 Schmid–Richter
Germany 1942
White to play and win

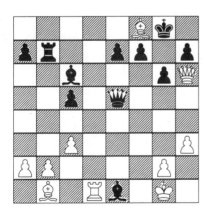

195 Bartrina–Ghitescu
Olot 1974
White to play and win

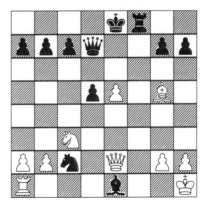

196 Tal–Miller
Los Angeles 1988
White to play and win

Solutions

193 1 ... ♘c1! (threatening 2 ... ♛d1 mate) 2 ♘d4 ♛b5+ 3 ♔g1 (3 ♔e1 ♖xd4; 3 ♘xb5 ♖d1 mate) 3 ... ♖xd4 4 cxd4 ♘e2+ 5 ♔f1 ♘g3+ 6 ♔g1 ♛f1+ 7 ♖xf1 ♘e2 and suddenly a smothered mate appears. **5 points**.

194 1 ♛h6+! ♔xh6 2 hxg6+ ♔g5 (2 ... ♔g7 3 ♖xh7 mate) 3 ♖h5+ ♔xh5 4 f4+ ♘xe2 5 ♘f6+ ♔h6 6 ♖h1+ ♔g7 7 ♘e8+ ♖xe8 8 ♖xh7+ ♔f8 or ♔xf6 9 ♖xf7 mate. **10 points**. You have incredibly good visualisation if you saw all this from the board!

195 1 ♗g7! (1 ♖d8 ♗f2+ 2 ♔xf2 ♖xb2+ wins for Black) 1 ... ♗f2+ (1 ... ♔xg7 2 ♖d8+) 2 ♔f1 (not 2 ♔h1 ♗xg2+ 3 ♔xg2 ♛g3+ 4 ♔f1 ♛g1+ 5 ♔e2 ♖xb2+) 2 ... ♗b5+ (2 ... ♗xg2+ 3 ♔xf2 ♖xb2+ 4 ♖d2 etc.) 3 ♔xf2 ♛e2+ 4 ♔g3 ♛xd1 5 ♗h8 ♛d6+ 6 ♔f2 ♔xh8 7 ♛f8 mate. **5 points**, but only if you calculated up to 5 ♗h8!

196 1 e6 ♛d6 (intending to exploit White's back rank with 2 ... ♛e5!) 2 ♘b5 ♛e5 3 h4 (so if 3 ... ♛xe2? 4 ♘c7 mate) 3 ... ♛g3 4 ♖d1 (threatening 5 ♖xd5, 5 ♖d3) 4 ... ♖f2 (4 ... c6 5 ♖d3 ♛b8 6 ♖f3 wins) 5 ♛xf2 ♗xf2 6 ♖xd5 is decisive. A bit unfair only to give **5 points** for this spot of Tal magic. Full credit if you saw as far as 3 h4.

A very difficult set. 25 points maximum. *Deduct* 1 point for each two minutes over thirty five minutes.

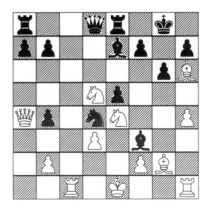

197 **Agdestein–
    Polugayevsky**
Haninge 1988
White to play and win

198 **Achang–Rodriguez**
Pinal Del Rio 1987
White to play and win

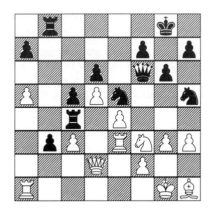

199 **Chiburdanidze–Goldin**
Palma de Mallorca
Black to play and win

200 **Plaskett–Hawelko**
Groningen 1978/79
White to play and win

Solutions

197 1 ♕xe8+! ♕xe8 2 ♘4f6+ ♗xf6 3 ♘xf6+ ♔h8 4 ♘xe8 ♗xg2 5 ♘f6 ♗xh1 6 ♖c7 followed by ♖xf7 and ♖xh7 mate. **5 points**. Black gets caught in a mating net. A knight check on f6 on move 1 would transpose.

198 1 ♘f5+ gxf5 (1 ... ♔h8 2 ♕f7 gxf5 3 ♗xh6 ♘xh6 4 ♘g6+ wins) 2 ♗b3 ♕xa1 3 ♕xg8+ ♗xg8 (3 ... ♖xg8 4 ♗xh6+ ♔h8 5 ♘f7 mate) 4 ♗xh6+ ♔h8 5 ♗xf8+ ♗h7 6 ♘g6 mate. **5 points** for this or the even prettier 1 ♕xg8+ ♔xg8 — on other recaptures 2 ♘f5+ mates — 2 ♗b3+ c4 3 ♗xc4+ ♔g7 4 ♖xa5 with a winning position.)

199 1 ... ♖a4 2 ♖xa4 b2 3 ♖e1 b1=♕ 4 ♖xb1 (4 ♘xe5 ♕b3 5 ♘d7 ♕fxc3) 4 ... ♖xb1+ 5 ♘e1 ♘d3 6 ♕xd3 ♖xe1+ 7 ♔g2 ♖xh1 8 e5 (8 ♔xh1 ♕xf2 followed by ...♘xg3+) 8 ...♖h2+ White resigned. **5 points**. Black is doing very nicely anyway, but the surest win here is to give up the passed pawn to deflect White's defenders from the kingside.

200 1 f5 hxg4 2 fxe6 gxf3 3 ♖xf3 ♘xe5 4 ♗b5+ ♔e7 (4 ...♗c6 5 ♕xe5 ♗xe5 6 ♗xc6+ is decisive.) 5 ♗g5+ f6 6 ♕xe5 ♖h5 7 ♗d7 ♖a6 (7 ... ♖xg5+ 8 ♕xg5 fxg5 9 ♖f7 mate) 8 ♖af1 ♕f8 9 h4 (threatening 10 ♕c7) ♖xg5+ 10 hxg5 fxe5 11 ♖xf8 ♗xf8 12 ♖f7+ wins. A very impressive breakthrough combination with several problem-like themes. **10 points** for seeing as far as 7 ♗d7, **8 points** for seeing as far as 6 ♕xe5. **6 points** for choosing 3 exf7+; you are probably winning, and certainly better, but Black has chances to struggle.

25 points maximum. *Deduct* 1 point for each minute over thirty-five minutes.

Now add up your score!

Scores

In each chapter the maximum score is 100 points. In the early chapters, master players would be expected to score close to 100%. Later chapters become more difficult.

Do not forget to take into account time penalties!

Chapter	Master	FIDE rated	Expert	Good club player	Club player	Average player	Social player
1 (1-20)	95+	85-95	75-85	65-75	55-65	40-55	up to 40
2 (21-40)	95+	85-95	75-85	65-75	55-65	40-55	up to 40
3 (41-56)	90+	80-90	70-80	60-70	50-60	35-50	up to 35
4 (57-72)	90+	80-90	70-80	60-70	50-60	35-50	up to 35
5 (73-88)	90+	80-90	70-80	60-70	50-60	35-50	up to 35
6 (89-104)	90+	80-90	70-80	60-70	45-60	30-45	up to 30
7 (105-120)	90+	80-90	70-80	55-70	45-60	30-45	up to 30
8 (121-136)	90+	80-90	70-80	55-70	45-60	25-45	up to 25
9 (137-152)	85+	75-85	65-75	50-65	35-50	25-35	up to 25
10 (153-168)	85+	75-85	65-75	50-65	35-50	20-35	up to 20
11 (169-184)	85+	75-85	65-75	50-65	35-50	20-35	up to 20
12 (185-200)	85+	75-85	65-75	50-65	35-50	20-35	up to 20

Rating equivalents:

	International Elo	USCF	BCF
Master	2400+	2500+	225+
FIDE rated	2200-2400	2300-2500	200-225
Expert	2000-2200	2100-2300	175-200
Good Club Player	1800-2000	1900-2100	150-175
Club Player	1600-1800	1500-1700	125-150
Average	1400-1600	1500-1700	100-125
Social player	1400 or below	1500 or below	100 or below